REVELATION

God's Gift of
Hope

A Guided Discovery for Groups and Individuals

Kevin Perrotta

LOYOLA PRESS.
A JESUIT MINISTRY
Chicago

LOYOLA PRESS.
A JESUIT MINISTRY

3441 N. Ashland Avenue
Chicago, Illinois 60657
(800) 621-1008
www.loyolapress.com

Nihil Obstat
Reverend John G. Lodge, S.S.L., S.T.D.
Censor Deputatus
October 5, 1999

Imprimatur
Most Reverend Raymond E. Goedert, M.A., S.T.L., J.C.L.
Vicar General
Archdiocese of Chicago
October 7, 1999

The *Nihil Obstat* and *Imprimatur* are official declarations that a book is free of doctrinal and moral error. No implication is contained therein that those who have granted the *Nihil Obstat* and *Imprimatur* agree with the content, opinions, or statements expressed.

The Scripture quotations contained herein are from the New Revised Standard Version Bible: Catholic Edition, copyright © 1993 and 1989 by the Division of Christian Education of the National Council of Churches of Christ in the U.S.A. Used by permission. All rights reserved. Subheadings in Scripture quotations have been added by Kevin Perrotta.

The autobiographical reflections of Jean Marie Rencher (p. 23) originally appeared in *New Covenant*, October 1986, 20–21.

The autobiographical reflections of Kathleen Norris (p. 47) originally appeared in *The Cloister Walk* (New York: Riverhead Books, 1996), 210–20.

Information about Nijole Sadunaite (p. 71) can be found in Michael Bordeaux, *Land of Crosses* (Devon: Keston College, 1979).

The Latin text of Bede's commentary on Revelation (p. 83) can be found in *Patrologia Latina*, edited by J. Migne. Translation by Kevin Perrotta.

The eyewitness account of the martyrdom of Polycarp, bishop of Smyrna (p. 86), can be found in *The Apostolic Fathers II*, Loeb Classical Library 25 (Cambridge: Harvard University Press, 1913), 307–45.

Interior design by Kay Hartmann/Communique Design
Illustration by Charise Mericle Harper

ISBN-13: 978-0-8294-1435-6; ISBN-10: 0-8294-1435-5

Printed in the United States of America
    12 13 14 15 16 17 18 Bang 15 14 13 12 11 10 9 8 7 6

Contents

How to Use This Guide

You might compare this booklet to a short visit to a national park. The park is so large that you could spend months, even years, getting to know it. But a brief visit, if carefully planned, can be worthwhile. In a few hours you can drive through the park and pull over at a handful of sites. At each stop you can get out of the car, take a short trail through the woods, listen to the wind blowing in the trees, get a feel for the place.

In this booklet we'll drive through the Revelation of John, making half a dozen stops along the way. At those points we'll proceed on foot, taking a leisurely walk through the selected passages. The readings have been chosen to take us to the heart of the message John conveys in this letter.

After each discussion we'll get back in the car and take the highway to the next stop. "Between Discussions" pages summarize the portions of Revelation that we will pass along the way.

This guide provides everything you need to explore Revelation in six discussions—or on your own. The introduction on page 6 will prepare you to get the most out of your reading. The weekly sections feature key passages from John's Revelation, with explanations that highlight what his words mean for us today. Equally important, each section supplies questions that will launch you into fruitful discussion, helping you both to explore Revelation for yourself and to learn from one another. If you're using the booklet by yourself, the questions will spur your personal reflection.

Each discussion is meant to be a *guided discovery*.

Guided. None of us is equipped to read the Bible without help. We read the Bible *for* ourselves but not *by* ourselves. Scripture was written to be understood and applied in and with the church. So each week "A Guide to the Reading," drawing on the work of both modern biblical scholars and Christian writers of the past, supplies background and explanations. The guide will help you grasp John's message. Think of it as a friendly park ranger who points out noteworthy details and explains what you're looking at so you can appreciate things for yourself.

Discovery. The purpose is for *you* to interact with John's letter—and with Jesus, the Lamb of God, whom John describes.

"Questions for Careful Reading" is a tool to help you dig into the book and examine it carefully. "Questions for Application" will help you discern what it means for your life here and now. Each week concludes with an "Approach to Prayer" section that helps you respond to God's Word. Supplementary "Living Tradition" and "Saints in the Making" sections offer the thoughts and experiences of Christians past and present in order to show you what Revelation has meant to others—so that you can consider what it might mean for you.

How long are the discussion sessions? We've assumed you will have about an hour and a half when you get together. If you have less time, you'll find that most of the elements can be shortened somewhat.

Is homework necessary? Before you begin, we strongly suggest you read the introductory article, "Getting Your Bearings in This Mysterious Book," on page 6. As you go through the six weeks, you will get the most out of the discussions if you read the weekly material in advance of each meeting. But if participants are not able to prepare, have someone read the "What's Happened" and "Guide to the Reading" sections aloud to the group at the points where they occur in the weekly material.

What about leadership? If you happen to have a world-class biblical scholar in your group, by all means ask him or her to lead the discussions. But in the absence of any professional Scripture scholars, or even accomplished biblical amateurs, you can still have a first-class Bible discussion. Choose two or three people to be facilitators, and have everyone read "Suggestions for Bible Discussion Groups" before beginning (page 92).

Does everyone need a guide? a Bible? Everyone in the group will need their own copy of this booklet. It contains the sections of Revelation that are discussed, so a Bible is not absolutely necessary—but you should have at least one Bible on hand for your discussion. (See page 96.)

How do we get started? Take a look at the suggestions for Bible discussion groups (page 92) and individuals (page 95).

D iscipleship certainly seems complicated in today's world. Being a Christian must have been simpler when it meant hiking around Galilee with Jesus."

"In theory, there are points where Christianity conflicts with the business world. In practice it's almost always unclear where those points are or what to do about them."

"I believe Jesus is Lord. But downtown on a Monday morning, it's not easy to see what that means."

Would you be surprised if I told you these scraps of conversation were overheard among parishioners at, say, St. Hugo's Church in Bloomfield, Michigan, an affluent Detroit suburb? Probably not. What if I told you they were remarks made by Christians less than a century after Jesus' death and resurrection?

Actually, the quotes are fictional. But toward the end of the first century A.D., some Christians might have voiced such sentiments, for example, those living in the cities of a region called Asia (present-day western Turkey). Asian cities were competitive, status-conscious, multicultural urban centers closely linked to international trade and finance. Christians in these cities encountered opportunities and difficulties absent from the Jewish villages where Jesus spent most of his life. Christian residents faced difficult questions about how to live as Jesus' followers when business, politics, and culture were based on pagan values. Leading a Christian life in these cities was as challenging as getting a PC program to run on a Macintosh computer.

To some of these urban Christians, around the year 90, a respected Church leader named John wrote a lengthy pastoral letter—the letter we know today as Revelation, or the Apocalypse. The author was probably not the man who wrote the Gospel of John, although there is no way to be certain.

Christians at that time already followed the custom of gathering on Sunday to celebrate the Eucharist, usually in the spacious home of a wealthier member of the community. When John's letter arrived, the recipients probably read it aloud the next Sunday at their celebration of the Eucharist. When we read Revelation today, we are like guests of those early Christians, sitting next to them as they listen to John's words.

We listen because John's letter speaks to us also. He did not write a list of how-tos for Christian life in first-century Asia ("what kind of inn to avoid when you have to travel as a wine merchant," "how to choose a not-too-pagan Greek grammar school for your children"). Specific advice like that would be of little use to us. John recognized that his Christian friends needed a fresh, basic vision of Christianity, and he gave it to them. His message continues to give us the big picture of Christianity as we live amid complexities and ambiguities today.

Revelation contains a message for us, but we must work to get hold of it. John alludes to problems his readers face without bothering to describe them, since they were familiar to his recipients. John also uses an almost psychedelic picture language, different from anything in modern writing. To grasp his message, then, we have to know a little about the social background and about John's style of writing. These are the matters we will look at in the remainder of this introduction. I apologize for its length, but without sufficient introduction, Revelation will remain mystifying, even misleading.

Background. The recipients of the letter lived in seven cities in Asia (1:4, 11). Some of these cities were large for their time, with up to a couple of hundred thousand inhabitants. In all of them Christians were a small minority. Except for some Christians and Jews, the inhabitants practiced a blended paganism in which local deities mingled with Greek gods—Greek being the international culture of the day. Ever since the region had become part of the Roman Empire more than a century before, the citizens had also venerated the Roman emperors as divine.

Pagan religion permeated these ancient cities the way advertising permeates ours. As a resident you would encounter paganism at every turn. Religious statues were set up in houses and on streets and in the places where people conducted business, ran the government, studied, worked out, and bathed. If you were a merchant or a craftsman, you belonged to a business association whose social events featured acts of gratitude to the organization's patron god. If you became sick, the clinic you went to was located in a shrine to the healing god. If you bought meat in the marketplace, you might be buying portions left over from pagan sacrifices.

If as a Christian you tried to distance yourself from all this homage to pagan gods, you would offend your relatives, neighbors, and the people you worked for or did business with. They would think you were antisocial and unpatriotic; they might even call you an atheist. They would pressure you to go along with the paganism they considered normal. Refusal could hurt you financially or get you sent into exile—as happened to John (1:9; Patmos was an island used as a place of exile). You might even be killed (2:13).

All Christians looked for ways to worship only the one God while getting along in the world. But they held a range of views about what degree of accommodation with pagan society was legitimate. Some were rigorous in drawing the line; they insisted on making hard choices and accepting the consequences. Others advocated a relaxed approach to the pervasive paganism.

In John's view, the Christians' eternal destiny and the integrity of the Christian communities were at stake in this confrontation with pagan culture. He wrote to urge his Christian friends to be faithful, public witnesses to Jesus. Addressing both the rigorous and the relaxed, John made a two-pronged appeal. To those suffering losses for their loyalty to Jesus, John offered the assurance that sharing in Jesus' sufferings means sharing in Jesus' conquest of death. John warned too-accommodating Christians that compromising with paganism would destroy their relationship with Jesus. Convinced that hostility toward Christianity was going to increase, John wished to encourage faithful but fearful Christians and to put a healthy fear into those who were drifting along complacently with the pagan culture.

John did not try to settle the many practical issues his readers encountered in their pagan cities. His goal was motivational rather than directive. John pursued his goal by laying before his readers a series of visions that reveal the underlying conflict between the gospel and paganism. Essentially the visions show the coming of God's kingdom in symbolic form. John hoped that if his readers gained a clearer understanding of God's action, they would be better prepared to cooperate with it. Seeing where they stood in the big picture, they would be able to take their stand as Christians in their everyday circumstances. If they were sufficiently motivated, they would be able to discern for themselves the requirements of Christian life in their particular situations.

John's style of writing. John's method of communicating divine revelation through symbolic visions is called *apocalyptic,* which means "revelatory." Apocalyptic writing was widely used by Jews and then Christians in the period shortly before and after the time of Jesus. This apocalyptic approach was understandable to John's first readers, but before long, apocalyptic writing went out of style. Less than two hundred years after John, a bishop named Methodius, who lived in the same part of the world, wrote a story in which a character declares that Revelation is full of "tremendous obscurities." She says, "To find the interpretation and explain it to you is beyond my powers" (although she goes on to offer an interpretation anyway).

Like other apocalyptic writings, Revelation abounds with grandiose and bizarre apparitions. Symbolic numbers, colors, clothes, and substances mysteriously recur in ever new combinations. Scenes shift abruptly. Anatomically improbable creatures lumber into view. It is little wonder that readers from Methodius's time until today have struggled to make sense of John's turbulent stream of images.

We will explore the meaning of some of John's images in the "Guide to the Reading" sections—without trying to explain every last detail.

The time or times John's visions refer to. John seems to describe the last days. But is John writing only about the end of the world? And is he saying it will come soon? The answers come into focus if we consider Jewish expectations and how Jesus fulfilled them.

In Jesus' day many Jews expected God to establish his kingdom in the world. They based their hopes on the way that God had cared for them in the past and on what he had promised through the prophets. Jews expected God to forgive their sins and bring home the scattered twelve tribes of Israel once more, just as he had led Israel in the exodus from Egypt. God would send a messiah, defeat his political enemies, and vindicate his people. God would restore the Jerusalem temple and dwell there in a splendid new way among his people in the Promised Land. There would be tribulation, judgment, resurrection, and lasting peace.

Jews disagreed about how, when, and in what sequence these events would occur and exactly what they would look like. Generally, however, they expected them to occur in the present world. They did not think that the world was about to end, only that the present age was about to end and a final, wonderful period was about to begin. They called this final period "the last days" or "the end of days" (Daniel 10:14).

Jesus proclaimed, "The kingdom of God has come near" (Mark 1:15). This announcement signaled that his people's expectations were about to be fulfilled. But Jesus indicated that he brought God's kingdom in an unexpected way. He gathered Israel's twelve tribes by calling twelve disciples to *himself;* he declared *himself* to be the temple in which God would dwell among his people. Jesus redefined Israel's enemies: not principally the Romans, but sin, Satan, and death. And Jesus announced a shocking strategy for overcoming these enemies: dying on a cross and rising from the dead! In this way he would inaugurate the messianic reign, although some aspects of God's promises would be fulfilled not in the present world but in an eternal kingdom.

After Jesus' ascension his followers realized that, in an unexpected fashion, the messianic kingdom *has now come.* As they put it, "Jesus *is* Lord!" (see Acts 2:36; Philippians 2:5–11). By his death and resurrection, the last days *have arrived* (see Acts 2:17; 1 Corinthians 10:11; Hebrews 1:2). But these last days are not a time for Israel to enjoy peace in the Promised Land and to worship God in a renewed Jerusalem temple. The messianic age is marked by the gift of God's Spirit (Acts 1:1–8; 2:16–21, 33–38). Instead of remaining in the Promised Land in earthly peace, God's people must now go forth to bear witness to God's reconciliation to the whole world—a mission that entails suffering as well as blessing. The gathering of Israel, the availability of God's forgiveness, God's dwelling among his people—all these promises are now being fulfilled as people everywhere come to believe in Jesus. At the end of these last days the Lord will return to give final judgment, resurrection, and eternal reward.

With this understanding of Jesus and the last days, let's go back to Revelation. We can see now that just because John presents visions of the last days does not mean he is speaking only about the end of the world. Like the rest of the early Church, John believed that humanity began to live in the last days when Jesus died and rose from the dead. Thus many of John's visions concern not the end of the world but the entire period from Jesus' resurrection to his return —that is, the last days, in which we now live. Our readings in Weeks 1, 3, and 4 will be samples of these visions concerning the present age.

As you will see, John does use end-of-the-world imagery. This technique creates a tremendous sense of urgency— undoubtedly a deliberately planned effect. But biblical persons sometimes used end-of-the-world imagery not to speak about the end of the world but to show that an event in their own time had ultimate importance. For example, Peter employed such imagery on Pentecost to express the cosmic significance of the gift of the Spirit (Acts 2:19–20).

In addition to references to the present period of history, some of John's visions look back to the event that inaugurated the last days: Jesus' death and resurrection. We will look at a couple of these visions in Weeks 2 and 4. Other visions look forward to the final judgment by which God will bring the last days to an end (Weeks 3 and 5). Finally, some visions give us a glimpse of the eternal kingdom after the end of the world (Weeks 3 and 6).

Because John is the only New Testament author to write mainly in an apocalyptic style, his message may seem different from that of the other writers of the New Testament. But in reality his book is simply a variation on central New Testament themes. The New

Testament writers describe the unexpected way that God has brought his kingdom through Jesus. John illustrates this through a wide range of symbolic images. New Testament authors demonstrate that Jesus fulfills the promises God made to Israel. John does this too, by weaving together many allusions to the Old Testament, especially allusions to God's judgment, the gathering of the twelve tribes, and God's presence with his people in a restored temple. Finally, like other New Testament authors, John attempts to bring home to his readers what all of this means for them in their particular situation.

John's visions were intended to speak to his urban Christian friends about their powerlessness in a pagan society dominated by the Roman emperor. John showed that the real emperor of the universe is Jesus. He portrayed the defeat of the ferocious evils that sought to deceive and destroy Christians. He showed them that, like Jesus, Christians conquer evil when they choose to be "conquered" by persecution rather than abandon their testimony to God's love. To stir their hope, John gave them an insight into the wonderful life that God prepares for those who are faithful.

John tailored his message to the readers of his day. Thus he did not fill his letter with specific references to the twentieth and twenty-first centuries, as some people suppose. What good would that have been to his readers? A message loaded with cryptic references to oil wells, ballistic missiles, China, and Russia would not have been much of a word of the Lord to *them*. Jesus commissioned John to give his readers a message to keep (1:1–3; 22:7), that is, a message to live by, not one to put in an archive for use two thousand years later.

A question about timing remains. Did John think his visions of the final judgment would be fulfilled in his own day? In other words, did he expect the end of the world at the end of the first century? At first John's letter may give the impression that he thought the end of the world was imminent, but on closer examination the answer is not so simple.

John's visions shuttle back and forth between past, present, and future with few indicators regarding which historical times they correspond to. For example, in one vision John reports that five kings have passed from the scene, one is, and one is yet to come (17:10), but he does not say what historical moment, if any, this vision refers to.

John uses the word *soon* and speaks of brief periods, such as "forty-two months" (11:2). He says, "The time is near" (1:3). If taken literally, these terms would suggest that he expected the end of the world in the near future. But John's language is heavily symbolic. In any case, other symbols suggest that the end will not arrive for a long time. A "thousand years" must pass, and a huge number of martyrs' places—144,000—must be filled before the end (6:11; 7:4–9; 20:4).

John does communicate a conviction that age-old evils are reaching a climax in the idolatrous, materialistic, and unjust Roman Empire. But he does not close off the possibility that these evils may yet manifest themselves in other governments and economic systems in the future.

Thus John's letter continues to have meaning for us, who know that the last days have turned out to be a very long period indeed. What John says about the last days continues to give us insight into the spiritual dynamics of our world. This is the approach to interpreting Revelation that many Christians have taken since the time of St. Augustine in the fourth century, and it is the approach we will take in this booklet.

In closing, here are a few suggestions for getting the most out of your reading and discussion.

Focus on the main issues. Don't get lost in the details. In Revelation a single detail can be incredibly rich, and when the details are combined, the complexity is endless. Fight the temptation to get bogged down and bewildered.

Don't try to understand the entire book all at once. Avoid mental overload! Identify a few points, and ponder what they mean for you.

Ask the Holy Spirit to guide you. He was John's coauthor in the writing of this letter. Let him be your coreader also.

Week 1

HE KEEPS THE LAMPS BURNING

Questions to Begin

15 minutes
Use a question or two to get warmed up for the reading.

1   What images of Jesus in religious art (paintings, icons, statues, stained-glass windows) are particularly meaningful for you? Why?

2   What is your attitude toward reading and discussing the book of Revelation?
   ❑ Maybe I'll finally find out what 666 stands for.
   ❑ Who do we think we are? Isn't this the most difficult book in the Bible?
   ❑ I've always wanted to read Revelation for myself.
   ❑ I just hope no one in the group is going to try to preach their pet theories about the end of the world.
   ❑ With all the judgments and weirdness, is this really a book that Christians can benefit from reading?
   ❑ This promises to be really interesting!

Opening the Bible

5 minutes
Have someone in the group read "The Reading" aloud. (If participants have not already read "What's Happened," read that aloud also. Otherwise skip it.)

What's Happened

For the first reading of John's letter, the Christians he wrote to were gathered together for the Eucharist. His opening perfectly suited the liturgical setting. He blesses the liturgical reader and listeners and announces that they are about to hear a word from the Lord (1:1–3). He offers a prayer to Jesus before beginning (1:5–6).
He concludes with a solemn word from God, preparing his readers for an awesome message: " 'I am the Alpha and the Omega,' says the Lord God, who is and who was and who is to come, the Almighty" (1:8).

The Reading: Revelation 1:9–20; 2:18–29

A Vision of the Risen Lord

[9] I, John, your brother who share with you in Jesus the persecution and the kingdom and the patient endurance, was on the island called Patmos because of the word of God and the testimony of Jesus. [10] I was in the spirit on the Lord's day, and I heard behind me a loud voice like a trumpet [11] saying, "Write in a book what you see and send it to the seven churches, to Ephesus, to Smyrna, to Pergamum, to Thyatira, to Sardis, to Philadelphia, and to Laodicea."

[12] Then I turned to see whose voice it was that spoke to me, and on turning I saw seven golden lampstands, [13] and in the midst of the lampstands I saw one like the Son of Man, clothed with a long robe and with a golden sash across his chest. [14] His head and his hair were white as white wool, white as snow; his eyes were like a flame of fire, [15] his feet were like burnished bronze, refined as in a furnace, and his voice was like the sound of many waters. [16] In his right hand he held seven stars, and from his mouth came a sharp, two-edged sword, and his face was like the sun shining with full force.

[17] When I saw him, I fell at his feet as though dead. But he placed his right hand on me, saying, "Do not be afraid; I am the first and the last, [18] and the living one. I was dead, and see, I am alive forever and ever; and I have the keys of Death and of Hades. [19] Now write what you have seen, what is, and what is to take place after this.

20 As for the mystery of the seven stars that you saw in my right hand, and the seven golden lampstands: the seven stars are the angels of the seven churches, and the seven lampstands are the seven churches. . . .

A Report Card for the Church

2:18 "To the angel of the church in Thyatira write: These are the words of the Son of God, who has eyes like a flame of fire, and whose feet are like burnished bronze:

19 "I know your works—your love, faith, service, and patient endurance. I know that your last works are greater than the first. 20 But I have this against you: you tolerate that woman Jezebel, who calls herself a prophet and is teaching and beguiling my servants to practice fornication and to eat food sacrificed to idols. 21 I gave her time to repent, but she refuses to repent of her fornication. 22 Beware, I am throwing her on a bed, and those who commit adultery with her I am throwing into great distress, unless they repent of her doings; 23 and I will strike her children dead. And all the churches will know that I am the one who searches minds and hearts, and I will give to each of you as your works deserve.

24 "But to the rest of you in Thyatira, who do not hold this teaching, who have not learned what some call 'the deep things of Satan,' to you I say, I do not lay on you any other burden; 25 only hold fast to what you have until I come.

26 "To everyone who conquers and continues to do my works to the end,
I will give authority over the nations;
27 to rule them with an iron rod,
as when clay pots are shattered—
28 even as I also received authority from my Father. To the one who conquers I will also give the morning star. 29 Let anyone who has an ear listen to what the Spirit is saying to the churches."

10 minutes
Choose questions according to your interest and time.

1 In the first vision, what does Jesus do with his right hand (see 1:16–17)? What significance does the gesture in verse 17 gain from the fact that it is done with the same hand that performs the action in verse 16?

2 Some images are probably not meant to be pictured; for example, the sword coming from Jesus' mouth suggests the power of his words. What other images do you think should be understood for their meaning but not taken as pictorial?

3 Why does John make a point of referring to himself as "I, John, your brother who share with you in Jesus the persecution and the kingdom and the patient endurance" (1:9)?

4 What phrases or images from John's vision of Jesus in 1:9–20 reappear in the message to Thyatira (2:18–29)?

5 What images or ideas in this reading are puzzling or troubling? Why? Write them down and see whether they become clearer through reading further sections of Revelation and the guides to the reading.

A Guide to the Reading

If participants have not read this section already, read it aloud. Otherwise go on to "Questions for Application."

John draws a picture of Jesus that is strikingly different from the one we find in the Gospels. Is Jesus now a heavenly being with burning eyes and metal feet (1:14–15)?

No. John received a vision of Jesus so awesome as to be beyond description (see 1:17). Yet he must find human terms to convey it, so he communicates his vision symbolically. To represent Jesus' heavenly priesthood, John describes priestly clothing (1:13); for Jesus' divine splendor, white hair (1:14); for penetrating knowledge, fiery eyes (1:14); for unshakable stability, bronze feet (1:15); for supreme authority, a handful of stars (1:16). Each picture contributes an idea, and the ideas add up to a statement: having conquered death by his death and resurrection, Jesus shares the powers and majesty of God (1:18). The ideas fit together; the images, not quite. Jesus does not literally have white hair and a sword coming from his mouth. Yet the overall picture gives a sense of Jesus' grandeur. The picture stirs the imagination, even if it would resist being drawn.

Jesus calls himself "the first and the last" (1:17)—a phrase God applied to himself in the Old Testament (Isaiah 44:6). Biblical scholar George Beasley-Murray writes that Jesus is "the initiator of all things and the finisher of God's purposes for his creation."

Real estate agents say that three factors determine the market value of a house: location, location, location. Location also establishes the meaning of John's vision of Jesus. Jesus is surrounded by fixtures that support oil lamps (1:12). Priests kept the lamps burning in the Jerusalem temple. Jesus, then, is acting like a priest by taking care of the lamps, which here symbolize the churches (1:20). Jesus is about to give John messages and visions that will correct and encourage the churches. This will be Jesus' means of cleaning out dirty lamps, putting in new wicks, and filling the lamps with oil.

The vision shows that Jesus does not direct his people from a distance; he is among us, making sure the light of divine life in us continues to burn. John's vision symbolizes Jesus' promise "I am with you always, to the end of the age" (Matthew 28:20). Because Jesus faithfully tends his Church, the Church as a whole

can never go astray from God, despite the sins and failings of
its members.

Jesus commissions John to deliver messages to *seven*
churches (chapters 2–3). Throughout Revelation, the number seven
signals completeness, so to say the letters are directed
to seven churches means they are meant for the entire Church.

In the message to the Christians in Thyatira, we see Jesus'
fiery, all-knowing eyes probing the situation of a particular church
community (2:18, 23; compare 1:14). He finds not only faithful
service (2:19) but also a problem that needs to be set right.

Thyatira was a small-scale manufacturing and commercial
city. The craftsmen and merchants generally belonged to guilds, and
the social occasions sponsored by the guilds presented problems for
Christians because the celebrations involved offering homage to the
association's patron god and eating meat sacrificed to the god. They
sometimes also ended in sexual immorality. Could believers square
such practices with their commitment to Jesus?

It was bad for business to get excluded from the guild for
refusing to join in such pagan rites. So Christian businesspeople
must have felt relieved to hear the soothing advice that some Christians offered: "It's okay to go along with the pagan rites. They don't
mean anything anyway, since pagan gods do not really exist."

Jesus calls the community members who are giving this
compromising advice "Jezebel" (2:20). The name is used
symbolically; the original Jezebel was a queen of foreign origin who
led the Israelites into idolatry (1 Kings 16:31; 18:4, 13, 19). Here
"Jezebel" may refer to an individual. But "Jezebel," "those who
commit adultery with her" (2:22), and "her children" (2:23) may
simply be different ways of referring to a segment of the church.

If the compromisers do not change their ways, sickness
(2:22) and death (2:23) are in store for them. Just as the compromising behavior is described symbolically ("fornication" and
"adultery"—2:20–22—are often used in Revelation to refer to
idolatry), the references to punishment are also symbolic. Perhaps
sickness and death represent the compromisers' exclusion from the
Christian community and a rupture of relationship with Jesus.

Questions for Application

40 minutes
Choose questions according to your interest and time.

1 John says we receive a mixture of hardship, blessing, and help from God through belonging to Jesus (1:9). Describe a situation in which you experienced this combination. What have you learned from it?

2 When has Jesus brought you a message of encouragement? a message of correction? What effect did these messages have on you?

3 If you were to guess at the message of encouragement and correction Jesus would give you today, what do you think it would be? How do you think you should respond?

4 Is there a "Jezebel" voice in you that assures you certain sins are really okay? What arguments does it use? Do you listen?

5 When are you tempted to
downplay or even deny your faith
in Jesus?

6 What could you do to listen more
carefully to Jesus' words to you?

**"It is important to leave room for varied viewpoints. Often different
viewpoints complement each other."**

David Smith, *Guidebook for Bible Study*

Approach to Prayer

15 minutes
Use this approach—or create your own!

✦ Begin by having someone read this blessing to the group, adapted from Revelation 1:3:

Blessed is the one who reads aloud the words of the prophecy, and blessed are those who hear and who keep what is written. Blessed are those who listen for God's voice and respond to his words to them.

Let someone else read Revelation 1:17–18:

Do not be afraid; I am the first and the last, and the living one. I was dead, and see, I am alive forever and ever.

Then suggest this meditation:

Picture Jesus in the way that comes most naturally to you. Picture yourself with Jesus. Ask him to let you look at his evaluation of you, which he holds in his hand. Then talk it over with him.

Allow some minutes for silent reflection. End by praying the Our Father together.

Saints in the Making

Which Side of the Fence Was I Really On?

This section is a supplement for individual reading.

The last of Revelation's seven messages is addressed to the Christians in Laodicea. Jesus chastises them severely: "You are neither cold nor hot. . . . So, because you are lukewarm, . . . I am about to spit you out of my mouth" (3:15–16). The imagery probably alludes to the mineral-spring water that flowed through Laodicea. The brackish water, which caused violent retching, was lukewarm. By contrast, neighboring cities had healthful springs, one hot, the other cold. This image seems to refer to some condition in the Laodicean church that was spoiling the Christians' relationship with Jesus. Apparently the problem lay in their acceptance of Laodicea's complacent materialism (see 3:17).

How Christians today might respond to this message is suggested by the experience of a California woman named Jean Marie Rencher. She was dissatisfied with a lifestyle that kept her busy all the time but never left her feeling that she did anything well. As she mulled over her situation one day, she recalled Revelation 3:15–16, which had recently been read at Mass. "I had thought these harsh words at the time," she wrote. "Now I wondered if this was because they applied to me. I had been intending to be more committed to the Lord . . . after I got my own problems worked out. Now it seemed I had been given an ultimatum. Maybe I should decide which side of the fence I was really on."

Rencher rearranged her priorities. She quit her part-time job to have more time for her children, prayer, and needy neighbors. This commitment meant living on a smaller income, but she found that her family "was finding time to enjoy quiet pleasures."

The financial pinch drove Rencher to ask God for help. When one prayer was answered in an especially striking fashion, she and her husband found their faith in God reawakened. Wanting to reinforce their excitement "with something more substantial," they joined a Bible study and began to explore the meaning of the Mass.

Several years later, Rencher declared that her decision to respond to God's words in Revelation continued to deepen her relationships with her family, the Church, and God.

Between Discussions

In the remainder of chapters 2 and 3, John conveys messages from Jesus to Christian communities in six other cities of Asia. In all of them Christians face hostility. Jesus commends two communities for their faithfulness and warns of stiffer challenges to come (2:9–10; 3:8–10). He takes two communities to task for failing to correct members who are promoting compromise with the pagan culture. The compromisers, called false apostles, followers of Balaam, and Nicolaitans (2:2, 14–15), are probably like the Jezebel group at Thyatira (2:20). In one community, those who remain faithful to Jesus constitute only a minority (3:1–4). The seventh community has drifted into a condition of total compromise: it is "lukewarm" (3:16). Thus everywhere a battle rages for the soul of the Christian communities, sometimes most fiercely among those who are least aware of it. In the next seventeen chapters John will use flamboyant imagery to depict this spiritual conflict.

If we are to understand John, we must recognize the thoroughly symbolic nature of his visions. It would be almost impossible to emphasize this point too strongly. Numbers, times, places, names, behavior (fornication and prostitution, conquering and ruling, washing and singing), and things that happen to people (being burned up, gaining access to the tree of life) are all symbolic.

Indeed, there are multiple layers of symbolism. As we have seen, seven stars are said to be seven angels (1:20), but the angels themselves are symbolic—in this case representing the Church's heavenly nature and call. At just about every line of Revelation you could take a pen and write in the margin, "This is symbolic" and "This too is symbolic."

Therefore we must beware of taking *anything* in Revelation literally. For example, when we begin reading about God's sending judgments on the world (Week 3), we will need to keep in mind that the visions of wars, famines, and other catastrophes are not literal depictions. The visions do not convey *information* about historical events; they convey *meaning*. The visions help answer questions: What really happened when Jesus died on a cross? How does Jesus exercise his divine authority over the sinful human world? Where is God when Christians are persecuted by a pagan society? What is God doing when human beings destroy each other through warfare? What is the inner nature of the final fulfillment God prepares for us? The visions are neither sneak previews of tomorrow's news nor blueprints for the end of the world.

Nor do the visions contain tomorrow's news in code. Traffic signals are a kind of code. A green light simply means go. The greenness of the light does not say anything about the quality of going; the code of traffic signals does not suggest that the experience of going is greenish. Symbols, however, do make these kinds of connections. The roses I give my wife, for example, are symbolic. They are not a code telling her that today is our anniversary. Rather they are a symbol. Their loveliness represents her loveliness. Their freshness represents the freshness of my love for her. Their similarity to the roses I gave her the first time we went out reminds us of all the years since then.

We use symbols to speak about things too profound or complex or mysterious to be dealt with in a more direct fashion. My love for my wife is like that, so on our anniversary, I "say it with flowers." John is also dealing with matters that are profound, complex, and mysterious: Jesus' negation of death by his death, martyrs' entry into eternal life through being crushed by a hostile world, the victory of God's self-sacrificing love over self-aggrandizing human evil. John has said it not with flowers but with thrones, trumpets, kings, women, fire, and precious stones.

If Revelation were a prediction in code, it would be a self-defeating attempt at communication. John would have done better to decode the visions himself and tell us what they mean. That would have saved a lot of confusion. But his language is symbolic, and thus deeply instructive. John uses fire, for example, as a symbol of God's judgment. Since it is a symbol, it tells us no more about the literal nature of God's judgment than roses tell us about the literal nature of marriage. Yet as a symbol, fire conveys something we need to know: coming under God's judgment, like getting burned, is painful. The symbol gives us a sense of how strongly and instinctively we should seek to avoid that judgment.

THE LAMB ASCENDS THE THRONE

Questions to Begin

15 minutes
Use a question or two to get warmed up for the reading.

1 If there is music in heaven, what kind would you particularly look forward to hearing? What instrument would you like to play?

2 If there are living creatures besides humans and angels in heaven, what kinds do you hope are there? What kinds do you hope are left out?

Opening the Bible

5 minutes
Have someone in the group read "The Reading" aloud.

The Reading: Revelation 4:1–5:13

The Center of Reality

1 After this I looked, and there in heaven a door stood open! And the first voice, which I had heard speaking to me like a trumpet, said, "Come up here, and I will show you what must take place after this." 2 At once I was in the spirit, and there in heaven stood a throne, with one seated on the throne! 3 And the one seated there looks like jasper and carnelian, and around the throne is a rainbow that looks like an emerald. 4 Around the throne are twenty-four thrones, and seated on the thrones are twenty-four elders, dressed in white robes, with golden crowns on their heads. 5 Coming from the throne are flashes of lightning, and rumblings and peals of thunder, and in front of the throne burn seven flaming torches, which are the seven spirits of God; 6 and in front of the throne there is something like a sea of glass, like crystal.

Around the throne, and on each side of the throne, are four living creatures, full of eyes in front and behind: 7 the first living creature like a lion, the second living creature like an ox, the third living creature with a face like a human face, and the fourth living creature like a flying eagle. 8 And the four living creatures, each of them with six wings, are full of eyes all around and inside. Day and night without ceasing they sing,

"Holy, holy, holy,
the Lord God the Almighty,
who was and is and is to come."

9 And whenever the living creatures give glory and honor and thanks to the one who is seated on the throne, who lives forever and ever, 10 the twenty-four elders fall before the one who is seated on the throne and worship the one who lives forever and ever; they cast their crowns before the throne, singing,

11 "You are worthy, our Lord and God,
to receive glory and honor and power,
for you created all things,
and by your will they existed and were created."

Will God's Intentions Be Frustrated?

5:1 Then I saw in the right hand of the one seated on the throne a scroll written on the inside and on the back, sealed with seven seals; 2 and I saw a mighty angel proclaiming with a loud voice, "Who is worthy to open the scroll and break its seals?" 3 And no one in heaven or on earth or under the earth was able to open the scroll or to look into it. 4 And I began to weep bitterly because no one was found worthy to open the scroll or to look into it. 5 Then one of the elders said to me, "Do not weep. See, the Lion of the tribe of Judah, the Root of David, has conquered, so that he can open the scroll and its seven seals."

The Supreme Agent of God's Plans

6 Then I saw between the throne and the four living creatures and among the elders a Lamb standing as if it had been slaughtered, having seven horns and seven eyes, which are the seven spirits of God sent out into all the earth. 7 He went and took the scroll from the right hand of the one who was seated on the throne. 8 When he had taken the scroll, the four living creatures and the twenty-four elders fell before the Lamb, each holding a harp and golden bowls full of incense, which are the prayers of the saints. 9 They sing a new song:
> "You are worthy to take the scroll
>> and to open its seals,
> for you were slaughtered and by your blood you
>> ransomed for God
>> saints from every tribe and language and people and
>> nation;
> 10 you have made them to be a kingdom and priests
>> serving our God,
>> and they will reign on earth."

11 Then I . . . heard the voice of many angels . . . 12 singing . . . ,
> "Worthy is the Lamb that was slaughtered
> to receive power and wealth and wisdom and might
> and honor and glory and blessing!"

13 Then I heard every creature in heaven and on earth and under the earth and in the sea, and all that is in them, singing,
> "To the one seated on the throne and to the Lamb
> be blessing and honor and glory and might
> forever and ever!"

10 minutes
Choose questions according to your interest and time.

1 What does John first see in heaven? What might be the significance of this?

2 What is the main reason for the praise of the Enthroned One, that is, God, in chapter 4? for the praise of the Lamb, that is, Jesus, in chapter 5? Is there a similarity between what the Enthroned One has done and what the Lamb has done?

3 Compare 4:11 and 5:12, and reread 5:13. What might be the significance of the fact that the Lamb receives the same kind of praise as the Enthroned One?

4 What are the similarities and differences between the symbolic visions of Jesus in chapters 2 and 5? Be sure to consider what John hears as well as what he sees (1:18; 5:5). What aspects of Jesus does each vision emphasize?

5 As in last week's selection, some of John's images are hard to picture. What examples can you find here? What does this suggest about whether the visions are to be interpreted literally?

A Guide to the Reading

If participants have not read this section already, read it aloud. Otherwise go on to "Questions for Application."

T he Spirit takes John to heaven (4:2). In this thoroughly symbolic book, not even the word *heaven* is to be taken literally. Here *heaven* refers to a sphere of revelation, a dimension where John perceives the underlying structures and dynamics of the universe in symbolic form. Unlike the literal heaven, this symbolic heaven contains images of evil as well as good, since it reflects the world. Here John sees a fundamental reality, a problem, and a cosmic event.

A fundamental reality (4:1–11). John sees a throne, a symbol of absolute authority. He merely hints at the occupant by describing brilliant lights of various hues (4:3). God is the Enthroned One, who holds sovereignty over all.

Again, location is significant. The throne is surrounded by two sets of beings, the inner group of four probably representing all living creatures (4:6–8), the outer group of twenty-four probably representing the people of God (4:4). The arrangement shows God in the midst of his creation. While this is a heavenly vision, it reveals that God is not way off in a distant heaven or marginalized at the periphery of the universe. God rules at the center of reality.

Various details—the water, the lamps, the praises—allude to the furnishings and worship in the Jerusalem temple. Thus the vision indicates that God relates to the entire universe as he related to the temple: he fills it with his presence. In the universe, as in the temple, God reveals himself to his creatures and receives their praise.

Today few rulers sit on thrones, but the ruler of John's first-century world—the Roman emperor—certainly did. For John's listeners, his vision carried a striking message: the real emperor of the world is not Caesar but God.

A problem (5:1–3). The elders proclaim that all things serve God's purposes (4:11). But the symbolic heaven contains a sea, which, as becomes clear further on, is a symbol of the rebellion against God that is active in the world (4:6; 13:1; 21:1). Thus a problem is represented: How can God overcome evil so as to achieve his purposes for the universe? If God simply allows evil to operate, he will be a weak or unjust sovereign, a virtual accomplice in wrongdoing. But if he executes justice, he will destroy the very creation he intended for a better end.

The scroll in God's hand indicates that he has a solution to this dilemma (5:1), but he will not execute his plan by himself. He created the human race in his image and likeness as his representative to rule the earth, and only through the human race will he accomplish his plan. But all of us are sinners, so how can we implement the holy God's strategy for overcoming sin? "Who is worthy to open the scroll?" (5:2). British scholar G. B. Caird writes, "The divine decree waits . . . for the emergence of a human agent willing and worthy to put it into effect, one who will place himself unreservedly at the disposal of God's sovereign will."

A cosmic event (5:4–14). John now sees a symbolic enactment of what transpired when Jesus died on the cross and rose from the dead. Jesus appears as a lamb, slaughtered but alive again—symbolism that obviously refers to his death and resurrection. The Lamb bears the mark of his slaughter as a permanent sign of his willingness to undergo death in order to carry out God's plan for his sin-damaged creation. Jesus is qualified to be God's agent for creation because, as a human being, he placed himself unreservedly at the disposal of God's will. The Lamb steps forward to receive the scroll and take his place on God's throne (see 3:21).

The Lamb is powerful (its power is symbolized by horns—5:6) yet is a lamb nevertheless, a harmless creature rather than a predator. While the Lamb is also the Lion, a conquering animal (5:5), the Lamb has conquered not by killing but by giving his life for others as a sacrificial animal (5:9). At the heart of God's plan for overcoming evil and achieving his purpose for the universe—the plan the Lamb will now unfold—is self-sacrificing love and mercy. The Lamb's sacrifice destroys sin by forgiving it, enabling sinners to become priests in his presence (5:10). T. Francis Glasson writes, "This conception of the Lamb on the throne of the universe . . . suggests that love is the strongest power in the world."

Questions for Application

40 minutes
Choose questions according to your interest and time.

1 The great white throne is a first-century image of authority. What modern image could be used to convey a sense of God's authority over all?

2 John sees God at the center of reality. What does it mean to have a God-centered mentality? What does it mean to have God at the center of your life? How can you identify areas of your life where you are not letting God reign?

3 Describe a situation in which you became aware that God was unfolding his plan for your life (things just fell into place, you prayed for guidance and then became certain about what God wanted you to do, there was an extraordinary coincidence, etc.). How has this affected your relationship with God?

4 Does God unfold his purpose for your life as you, in Caird's words, place yourself "unreservedly at the disposal of God's sovereign will"? When have you tried to do this?

5 How could meditation on chapters 4 and 5 deepen your participation in the Eucharist? In what way are all Christians "a kingdom and priests serving our God" (5:10)?

"The ultimate goal of Bible study is application. God wants us to act on the Word, not just know its facts."

Neal F. McBride, *How to Lead Small Groups*

Approach to Prayer

15 minutes
Use this approach—or create your own!

✦   Pray the prayers in 4:8 and
4:11. Then give everyone an
opportunity to thank God for
particular things he has done.

Use this adaptation of the prayer
in 5:9–10:

Lord Jesus, you are worthy to be
praised, worthy to unfold God's
plan for our lives, because you
were slaughtered, and by your
blood you ransomed for God
[mention each member of the
group by name]. You have made
us to be a kingdom and priests
serving our God, living with you
forever.

Finally, pray together the prayers
in 5:12 and 5:13.

A Living Tradition

The Lord's Day

This section is a supplement for individual reading.

When we gather on Sunday to celebrate the liturgy, we do what Christians have been doing week after week since the days just after Jesus rose from the dead. In the New Testament we catch sight of Christians in Paul's day, only twenty years after Jesus' resurrection, getting together on the first day of the week (Acts 20:7–12; 1 Corinthians 16:2). Revelation, written a generation later, tells us what name Christians gave to this new weekly feast day: "the Lord's day" (1:10).

The first Christians were Jews, so they kept Saturday as the Sabbath, the Jewish day of rest. Jesus' resurrection revolutionized their understanding of God's purposes. Realizing that Jesus' resurrection was the fulcrum on which all history turned, they made the day on which he rose the new center of their week. About fifteen years after John wrote Revelation, a bishop named Ignatius of Antioch explained that Christians, having come to "a new hope," no longer observe the Sabbath but keep "the Lord's Day, the day on which our life has appeared."

It did not take long for Christians to realize that the first day of the week, on which Jesus rose from the dead, was also the day in Genesis 1 on which God began to create. A Christian spokesman named Justin, who died as a martyr in Rome around 165, explained to non-Christians that "we all gather on Sunday, for it is the first day, when God, separating matter from darkness, made the world; and on this same day Jesus Christ our savior rose from the dead." On the Lord's Day Christians celebrate both God's creation of the world and his new creation in Christ.

Since the Lord's Day followed the Sabbath, the seventh day, it was also the "eighth" day. In early Christian thinking, if the week represents time, the Lord's Day represents what follows time: eternity. Basil, a fourth-century bishop, explained that Sunday symbolizes "that day which will follow the present time, the day without end which will know neither evening nor morning. Sunday is the ceaseless foretelling of life without end which renews the hope of Christians and encourages them on their way." (See the *Catechism of the Catholic Church,* sections 2174–2188.)

Between Discussions

In the next chapters John narrates symbolic actions that originate in the heavenly throne room described in chapters 4 and 5. It will be helpful to have an understanding of the nature of this symbolic place.

G. B. Caird compares the heaven where John sees visions to a military control room: "Imagine a room lined with maps, in which someone has placed clusters of little flags. A man in uniform is busy moving some of the flags from one position to another. It is wartime, and the flags represent units of military command. The movement of the flags may mean one of two things: either that changes have taken place on the battlefield, with which the map must be made to agree, or that an order is being issued for troop movements, and the flags are being moved to the new positions the units are expected to occupy."

The enthronement of the Lamb (chapter 5) is a "movement of flags" of the first kind—a heavenly reflection of a change that has taken place on the earthly battlefield. It shows that by his death on Calvary Jesus has "conquered" (5:5), becoming Lord of the universe. In upcoming chapters many symbolic events are flag movements of the second kind. They represent orders God gives for "troop movements" on earth as he interacts with his sinful world.

The heaven of John's visions is a symbolic realm that shows the meaning and purpose of earthly events from God's point of view. There also exists, of course, a literal heaven—the actual, nonsymbolic, face-to-face presence of God. The symbolic heaven contains images of this literal heaven, such as a white throne and emerald light. Thus the symbolic heaven of chapters 4 and 5 is both a mirror reflecting earthly events "below" and a window giving a glimpse of literal heaven "above."

When we peer into the literal heaven through the symbolic window of chapters 4 and 5, we catch sight of an important reality: life in heaven is essentially liturgical. The creatures who see God are filled with wonder and awe, expressing their astonishment and appreciation with constant praise (4:8–11; 5:8–14).

Notice the similarities between the heavenly liturgy and the liturgy we celebrate. The heavenly acclamation "Holy, holy, holy" (4:8) is a refrain we use. The declaration "Worthy is the Lamb" (5:12) resembles the response at the beginning of the eucharistic prayer: "Truly it is right and fitting to give praise." The heavenly praises end with a cosmic "Amen!" (5:14)—the conclusion of our eucharistic prayer.

The heavenly beings praise God for creating the universe (4:11). They praise the Lamb for accepting death in order to rescue human beings from death. The Lamb has given his followers a "kingdom," that is, the conquest of death, and he has made his followers "priests," that is, people who stand before God (5:10). In our celebration of the Eucharist we too thank God for creation and for Jesus' death and resurrection.

Essentially, the liturgy in heaven and the liturgy on earth are not two different liturgies. There is one supreme liturgy in the entire universe: one perfect service to God, one total offering of self to God, one humble submission to God, one fully trusting acknowledgment that God is the giver of life. That is the liturgy Jesus offered on Calvary. That liturgy fills heaven with praise. That is the liturgy we offer on earth. (See the *Catechism of the Catholic Church*, sections 1136–1139.)

As we celebrate, we enter the liturgy in heaven. The twenty-four elders are a representation of the Church. They reflect our presence before God (compare Ephesians 2:4–7). In the Eucharist we join the angels and saints, singing, "Holy, holy, holy!"

As we worship God, we are changed. The worship of heaven reshapes our conception of God, the universe, and ourselves. Fostering this effect was one of John's goals in writing his letter. Biblical scholar Gregory Beale writes that "one of the purposes of the church meeting on earth in its weekly gatherings . . . is to be reminded of its heavenly existence and identity by modeling its worship and liturgy on the angels' and the heavenly church's liturgy of the exalted Lamb, as vividly portrayed in chapters 4 and 5." John wanted Christians to join in the heavenly worship and be changed by it. "This," says Beale, "is why scenes of heavenly liturgy are woven throughout the Apocalypse."

BENDING EVIL
TO HIS PURPOSES

Questions to Begin

15 minutes
Use a question or two to get warmed up for the reading.

1 What is the most surprising letter—or other message—you have ever received?

2 What kind of mail do you like to get?
❑ Letters from family and friends
❑ Postcards from people visiting exotic places
❑ Invitations to social events
❑ Funny greeting cards
❑ Notes of encouragement or friendship
❑ Fund-raising appeals
❑ Advertisements
❑ Bills
❑ E-mail

5 minutes
Have someone in the group read "The Reading" aloud.

The Reading: Revelation 6:1–17; 8:1

The Plan Begins to Unfold

[1] Then I saw the Lamb open one of the seven seals, and I heard one of the four living creatures call out, as with a voice of thunder, "Come!" [2] I looked, and there was a white horse! Its rider had a bow; a crown was given to him, and he came out conquering and to conquer.

[3] When he opened the second seal, I heard the second living creature call out, "Come!" [4] And out came another horse, bright red; its rider was permitted to take peace from the earth, so that people would slaughter one another; and he was given a great sword.

[5] When he opened the third seal, I heard the third living creature call out, "Come!" I looked, and there was a black horse! Its rider held a pair of scales in his hand, [6] and I heard what seemed to be a voice in the midst of the four living creatures saying, "A quart of wheat for a day's pay, and three quarts of barley for a day's pay, but do not damage the olive oil and the wine!"

[7] When he opened the fourth seal, I heard the voice of the fourth living creature call out, "Come!" [8] I looked and there was a pale green horse! Its rider's name was Death, and Hades followed with him; they were given authority over a fourth of the earth, to kill with sword, famine, and pestilence, and by the wild animals of the earth.

A Change of Scene

[9] When he opened the fifth seal, I saw under the altar the souls of those who had been slaughtered for the word of God and for the testimony they had given; [10] they cried out with a loud voice, "Sovereign Lord, holy and true, how long will it be before you judge and avenge our blood on the inhabitants of the earth?" [11] They were each given a white robe and told to rest a little longer, until the number would be complete both of their fellow servants and of their brothers and sisters, who were soon to be killed as they themselves had been killed.

A Vision of the End

[12] When he opened the sixth seal, I looked, and there came a great earthquake; the sun became black as sackcloth, the full moon became

like blood, [13] and the stars of the sky fell to the earth as the fig tree drops its winter fruit when shaken by a gale. [14] The sky vanished like a scroll rolling itself up, and every mountain and island was removed from its place. [15] Then the kings of the earth and the magnates and the generals and the rich and the powerful, and everyone, slave and free, hid in the caves and among the rocks of the mountains, [16] calling to the mountains and rocks, "Fall on us and hide us from the face of the one seated on the throne and from the wrath of the Lamb; [17] for the great day of their wrath has come, and who is able to stand?" . . .

[8:1] When the Lamb opened the seventh seal, there was silence in heaven for about half an hour.

Questions for Careful Reading

10 minutes
Choose questions according to your interest and time.

1 The visions following the first four seals form a group. What do these visions have in common?

2 Would a quart of wheat feed a family for a day (6:6)? What kind of economic circumstances are suggested by the price of grains here?

3 What contrasts can you find between the visions that follow the breaking of the fifth and sixth seals?

4 What picture of Jesus does this reading convey? How might this portrayal of Jesus fit together with the portrayals in chapter 1 and chapter 5?

5 What message do you think John was trying to bring to his readers through these visions?

A Guide to the Reading

If participants have not read this section already, read it aloud. Otherwise go on to "Questions for Application."

The Lamb opens the scroll: Jesus puts into operation God's plan for the universe during the period from his ascension to his return. Rather than peace and progress, however, destruction and death leap forth (6:1–8). What sort of divine plan is this? How can Jesus, who laid down his life for us, send starvation and epidemics (6:8)?

The horsemen symbolize war and its aftermath (famine and disease) and economic oppression (represented by the exorbitant prices for basic commodities in 6:6). Human beings cause these disasters. The horsemen are images of the consequences of our own evil choices. They symbolize what God has *not* created: sin. They represent the evil that infests God's creation.

Ultimately God will cleanse creation of these forces of death (20:14)—along with all those who have cast their lot with evil. In the meantime, however, God draws men and women to himself despite the evils of this age. God uses the painful consequences of our sins. The vision of the four horsemen being summoned and sent into the world shows the Enthroned One co-opting man-made evils, causing even rebellion against him to serve his saving plan.

The horsemen's springing forth as the Lamb breaks the seals is a way of showing that God is using man-made evils to carry out the Lamb's redemptive mission of bringing men and women into God's life (5:9). The Lamb who uses suffering in this way knows from his own experience how dreadful it can be to suffer the effects of human sin.

As God works through human evils to draw us to him, we experience his action in different ways, according to our posture toward him (see Wisdom 11:6–14; Sirach 39:25–40:5). If we have set ourselves against God's will, the painful consequences of sin prod us to repent. If we have been faithful to God, sorrows come as opportunities to draw even closer to him.

War and oppression are virtual constants throughout history. The four horsemen dispatched to inflict these evils do not represent four particular historical events. Rather they symbolize God's intention to harness these evils to serve his purposes through the entire period from Jesus' resurrection to his final return.

The breaking of the fifth seal shows another reality constant throughout history. Christians die for their faith and enter into God's presence (6:9–10).

The slaughtered Christians' prayer is not a cry for personal vengeance. The martyrs do not ask God to punish the particular people who tormented them but to bring judgment against "the inhabitants of the earth" (6:10). In Revelation this phrase means much the same as "the world" at certain other places in the New Testament, where it refers to sinful human society as a whole (1 John 2:15–17). *The inhabitants of the earth* is a collective term referring to a society that bases its security on the things of earth, refuses to trust in God, and has an unjust structure and worldly values. The martyrs' prayer means "Do not let sinful society triumph over good!" The urban Christians who first read the letter would have interpreted the martyrs' prayer as meaning "Bring down the pagan Roman Empire!" not "Punish all the Romans!"

We might compare sinful human society to a ship. The martyrs plead with God to launch a torpedo into it and send it to the bottom. Everyone on the ship will go down with it, but the martyrs are not asking that their persecutors be on board when that occurs. Indeed, rescuing people from the ship before it goes down is the reason God delays sinking it. He is allowing time for many of "the inhabitants of earth" to become "brothers and sisters" of the martyrs through Jesus. The reason God insists on his people being faithful, public witnesses to Jesus is he wants everyone to have the opportunity to get off the ship of rebellious human society before it meets its doom (6:11).

At the opening of the sixth seal, the scene shifts to the final judgment at the end of the world (6:12–17). For those who reject God's grace, Jesus' coming is terrifying. They cry, "Hide us from the . . . wrath of the Lamb" (6:16). Jesus is not filled with rage toward those who have rejected him. But, as Caird writes, those to whom sin has become second nature have developed a distorted perception of reality. "Faced with the love and forgiveness of the sacrificed Lamb, they can see only a figure of inexorable vengeance."

Questions for Application

40 minutes
Choose questions according to your interest and time.

1 How has God used the consequences of your sins to draw you closer to him? When have painful circumstances that were not your fault been an opportunity for you to experience God's presence and support?

2 When have you endured pain in the process of caring for someone else? What did you learn from that experience?

3 Pick a large-scale evil caused by human beings today. How might ordinary Christian people express self-sacrificial love and have a positive effect on that problem?

4 How might this reading affect your understanding of the petitions of the Our Father: "Our Father, who art in heaven, hallowed be your name. Your kingdom come, your will be done, on earth as it is in heaven"?

5 Are you somewhat afraid of God? How would you describe your fear? What is the reason for it? Is it a healthy awe of God's greatness?

"Good study facilitators are characterized by diligence in preparation, discipline in not answering their own questions, dependence on God's Word, delight in the contributions of others, and determination to be teachable and to grow."

Dan Williams, *Starting (& Ending) a Small Group*

Approach to Prayer

15 minutes
Use this approach—or create your own!

✦ Have each member of the group briefly mention a large-scale disaster that has been in the news. Then let one person pray this prayer:

Lord of all, your majesty and authority are great beyond our comprehension; equally beyond our understanding is the depth of your compassion and mercy. Lord, come to the aid of those who are enduring grief and loss. Do not let the downtrodden be crushed, but let the poor and needy praise your name. Use even sin and sorrow to accomplish good; put your grace in the midst of suffering. Guide us in showing your compassion.

End by praying the Our Father together.

Saints in the Making

Hearing Revelation As Poetry

This section is a supplement for individual reading.

Most of the text of John's letter marches down the page in regular blocks of type, like disciplined soldiers on parade. Revelation is mostly prose. Only a few lines here and there break free and dispose themselves in ragged verse. Yet by using symbolic scenes and striking, even shocking, pictures, John has chosen not to convince us by theological argument but to stir something in our hearts. To appreciate Revelation, we must read it as poetry. Better, we should listen to it being read aloud. Freed from the work of reading lines of print, our imagination can attend to the waves of images that John sends cascading over us.

The writer Kathleen Norris describes hearing Revelation read aloud at a monastery she visited: "Somehow, the simple magic of hearing the Bible read aloud opened my eyes to recognize the extent to which I had . . . allowed the resistance of the world to good to shake my faith in the kingdom of God." Norris found John's poetry an antidote to a worldview that was "terribly sophisticated but of little use in the long run."

She writes, "As I allowed the words of John's revelation to wash over me—to be repulsed, offended, attracted, and moved to tears of grief and anger, joy and wonder—my full sense of the sacredness of the world revived." She was struck by the way "all the angels of Revelation and the figure of Christ himself continually tell John, 'Do not fear.'" She found the angels of Revelation "refreshingly terrifying" in their calm execution of God's purposes. These were no "warm fuzzy gift-shop angels"!

If we read John's letter as poetry, we too will hear a melody of hope. John's voice is like the bird's in Emily Dickinson's poem:

> Hope is the thing with feathers
> That perches in the soul,
> And sings the tune without the words,
> And never stops at all,
> And sweetest in the gale is heard;
> And sore must be the storm
> That could abash the little bird
> That kept so many warm.

Between Discussions

A long with war and oppression, the four horsemen symbolize another evil caused by humans: persecution of Christians. The commission to the second horseman in particular implies this. He is told to "slaughter" (6:4)—a word with significant overtones. The word *slaughtered* has just been used to describe Jesus (5:6, 9), the faithful witness to God (3:14), and is almost immediately used again to describe Christians who have died as faithful witnesses to Jesus (6:9–11). Because the Lamb sends forth the horsemen, persecuted Christians can trust that the Lamb has a redemptive purpose for their suffering.

Chapter 7 takes a time-out from the breaking of the seals to say more about Christians who experience opposition for their faithfulness to Jesus in the "great ordeal" (7:14), which runs from Jesus' resurrection to his return. John hears of 144,000 of God's servants being sealed, or marked (7:1–8). Then he sees a huge crowd celebrating victory (7:9–17). Those John hears about and those he sees are one and the same group, as the Lion he heard about and the Lamb he saw were one person (5:5–6).

The men and women carry palm branches (7:9)—a sign of martyrdom. The Greek word *martus,* which gives us *martyr,* means "a witness in court." These men and women bore witness in the courtroom of the world that Jesus is Lord. Not only their palm branches but also they themselves are symbolic. As martyrs they represent not only those who have literally died for Jesus but also all who have lived as his witnesses in the world. They represent all of us. We are inherently a Church of witnesses, or martyrs.

Sealing and counting (7:1–8) express possession. Both actions signify that the followers of Jesus belong to God. He has us in his care. Indeed, without his protection we could not endure the difficulties we face. As biblical scholar Wilfrid Harrington points out, this protection guarantees not a painless life but an ultimately successful one: "The sealing of the elect recalls the immunity of the Israelites to the plagues that struck the Egyptians. John's unexpected twist is that his servants will be sealed for protection *through* the great tribulation. They achieve their victory, yes, but in the only Christian manner: 'love of life did not bring them to shrink from death' (12:11)."

From early times Christians applied the term *sealing* to baptism and confirmation. The Holy Spirit, given through immersing in water and rubbing with oil, protects and strengthens us, enabling us to be witnesses to Jesus in the face of difficulties. Early Christian teachers, such as fourth-century bishops John Chrysostom and Cyril of Jerusalem, spoke of these sacraments as a preparation for spiritual combat. The Syrian Christians who used one of the earliest church buildings ever discovered, in a town called Dura-Europos, had the same view: they decorated their baptistery with a fresco of David going to meet Goliath.

The roster of God's servants (7:4–8) suggests they are marshaled as an army. This army conquers with the Lamb and in the same way he did, by sharing in his faithfulness to God and his self-sacrificing love. As expressed in one of Scripture's most paradoxical images, these Christians "have washed their robes and made them white in the blood of the Lamb" (7:14). They have found forgiveness in Jesus' saving death. They have given testimony with him to God's love for a hostile world. They have endured with his strength. They have gained all by losing all with him. They share his conquest of death by having shared his dying. Robes "made white in the blood of the Lamb" are a symbol worth pondering!

Finally the Lamb breaks the seventh seal (8:1), and a vast silence follows—possibly symbolizing the beginning of a new creation. Rather than describing the new creation, John relates another series of seven—this time, seven trumpets—with another lengthy time-out before the last in the series (10:1–11:14). These visions cover the same ground as chapters 6 and 7: they symbolize further sufferings in the world during the course of history (chapters 8–9) and the Church's continued witness to Jesus (chapter 11). Of particular note in these visions is God's offer of forgiveness and people's choice to repent or not (9:20–21; 11:7–10).

THE LADY AND THE DRAGON

Questions to Begin

15 minutes
Use a question or two to get warmed up for the reading.

---

1   The lady in this reading bears a Son who fulfills prophetic expectations. Considering your parents' expectations for you, how might they think about what you have done with your life so far?
❑ I've pretty much met their expectations.
❑ I've done better than they could have imagined.
❑ I've done something very different with my life than they expected.
❑ They're disappointed in me.
❑ They're disappointed in me— and for good reasons!
❑ I feel that their expectations of me were unrealistic.

---

2   Describe a situation in which you were a witness to Jesus at work or with friends.

Have someone in the group read "The Reading" aloud. (If participants have not already read "What's Happened," read that aloud also. Otherwise skip it.)

What's Happened

Angels blow trumpets to summon a second series of visions (chapters 8–11). Like the visions of seals being opened (chapters 6–7), these visions interpret history between Jesus' resurrection and the end of the world. There remains more to be said about this age, however, so chapter 12 returns to Jesus' resurrection and proceeds over the same ground once more, examining it from a different vantage point.

The Reading: Revelation 12:1–17

A Heavenly Woman and Her Royal Child

1 A great portent appeared in heaven: a woman clothed with the sun, with the moon under her feet, and on her head a crown of twelve stars. 2 She was pregnant and was crying out in birth pangs, in the agony of giving birth. 3 Then another portent appeared in heaven: a great red dragon, with seven heads and ten horns, and seven diadems on his heads. 4 His tail swept down a third of the stars of heaven and threw them to the earth. Then the dragon stood before the woman who was about to bear a child, so that he might devour her child as soon as it was born. 5 And she gave birth to a son, a male child, who is to rule all the nations with a rod of iron. But her child was snatched away and taken to God and to his throne; 6 and the woman fled into the wilderness, where she has a place prepared by God, so that there she can be nourished for one thousand two hundred sixty days.

The Overthrow of the Devil

7 And war broke out in heaven; Michael and his angels fought against the dragon. The dragon and his angels fought back, 8 but they were defeated, and there was no longer any place for them in heaven. 9 The great dragon was thrown down, that ancient serpent, who is called the Devil and Satan, the deceiver of the whole world—he was thrown down to the earth, and his angels were thrown down with him.

^{10} Then I heard a loud voice in heaven, proclaiming,

"Now have come the salvation and the power
and the kingdom of our God
and the authority of his Messiah,
for the accuser of our comrades has been thrown down,
who accuses them day and night before our God.
^{11} But they have conquered him by the blood of the Lamb
and by the word of their testimony,
for they did not cling to life even in the face of death.
^{12} Rejoice then, you heavens
and those who dwell in them!
But woe to the earth and the sea,
for the devil has come down to you
with great wrath,
because he knows that his time is short!"

The Woman Persecuted and Protected

^{13} So when the dragon saw that he had been thrown down to the earth, he pursued the woman who had given birth to the male child. ^{14} But the woman was given the two wings of the great eagle, so that she could fly from the serpent into the wilderness, to her place where she is nourished for a time, and times, and half a time. ^{15} Then from his mouth the serpent poured water like a river after the woman, to sweep her away with the flood. ^{16} But the earth came to the help of the woman; it opened its mouth and swallowed the river that the dragon had poured from his mouth. ^{17} Then the dragon was angry with the woman, and went off to make war on the rest of her children, those who keep the commandments of God and hold the testimony of Jesus.

10 minutes
Choose questions according to your interest and time.

1 On the basis of the description of the dragon's activities in verses 9–10, what sorts of things does the water coming from the dragon's mouth in verse 15 probably symbolize?

2 Verse 17 says the dragon goes off "to make war" on the woman's other children. Again, judging from the description of the dragon in verses 9–10, what kind of demonic activity does this war probably symbolize?

3 After looking back at 3:21 and 5:6–7, who would you say the child in verse 5 is? Who, then, might the woman's other children be (verse 17)? What relationship do they have with the child in verse 5?

4 Sometimes the heavenly voice that John hears is the voice of God or the Lamb. Is this the case in verses 10–12?

5 Describe in your own words the characteristics of Christians mentioned in verses 11 and 17.

A Guide to the Reading

If participants have not read this section already, read it aloud. Otherwise go on to "Questions for Application."

The aspect that now comes to the fore is the demonic nature of the evil at work beneath the surface of human affairs. Demonic forces are symbolized by a dragon (chapter 12), who is soon accompanied by two deputy monsters (chapter 13). The three are an unholy trinity, an anti-God. Later an attractive prostitute joins them (chapter 17). Evil often looks good and even mimics God, yet behind its powerful and attractive masks, it is ugly and subhuman.

John's descriptions of the beasts combine traditional Jewish images for the devil with details suggestive of the Roman emperors. John's point is that age-old demonic powers were expressing themselves through the emperors. Acts of worship to the emperors seemed innocuous to some of John's readers. He wanted them to realize that this socially accepted idolatry was an alliance with deadly evil.

In the first vision (12:1–6), the woman represents God's people (12:1). Her heavenly radiance indicates their heavenly calling and protection (her twelve-starred crown alludes to the twelve tribes of Israel). Her child is the Messiah, who enters the world amid the sufferings of his people (12:2). The vision lacks imagery for Jesus' earthly life because the focus is not on his literal birth in Bethlehem but on his figurative birth on Calvary. In the ancient Near East, a king's enthronement was regarded as his day of birth, and Jesus' enthronement is precisely what John is concerned with. His message is that while Jesus' death looked like a total defeat, it was in fact the means by which Jesus was "snatched away" from defeat and placed on the throne of the universe (12:5).

A second vision explains what Jesus' enthronement means for us (12:7–12). John sees Satan being thrown out of heaven. Satan is viewed as the prosecutor, or "accuser" (12:10), who reminds God of our sins. The prosecutor is fired, and his position is eliminated because God has pardoned all the accused. Michael's ejection of Satan is not a second event separate from Jesus' death and resurrection. It is a heavenly symbol of an earthly reality: when Jesus died on Calvary, our sins were forgiven, and the accuser of sins was defeated. The game was over, so to speak, and we see the devil's piece being removed from the board. Jesus spoke of the same reality, although in less picturesque language (John 12:31).

When we are reconciled with God through Jesus, we are freed from all accusations, no matter how destructive and shameful our sins were. We now belong in God's presence because Jesus' death has put us there (see Romans 8:1). If guilty thoughts continue to plague us, we might picture God disposing of them the way Michael tosses the dragon out of heaven.

By his enthronement, Jesus has made a way for us into "the salvation and the power and the kingdom of our God" (12:10), that is, into life forever with God. Jesus has faithfully testified to God's love (3:14), even to the point of death. If we identify with Jesus and bear witness with him to God's love in this world, even to the point of death, then his saving death will remove everything in us that could separate us from God. We too will conquer death. This is the message of 12:10–12. These verses stand at the exact center of the Revelation. They express John's central appeal to us: Choose Jesus! Stand with him, no matter what the cost! Enter life with him!

Even though the devil can no longer accuse Jesus' followers of sin, he still has the power to cause us suffering and deceive us (12:9, 12–13, 15, 17). The protection of the woman in the desert (12:14–16) is an image of God's promise to enable his people— now meaning the Church—to be faithful to him as we pass through the difficulties of this world, just as he cared for the people of Israel when they traveled through the desert to the Promised Land. God's protection is a shield not from suffering (12:11) but from deceptions and temptations, symbolized here by the flood of false teaching that pours out of the dragon's mouth (12:15). The snake in Eden deceived the first woman, but the dragon will not succeed in leading astray this woman, who is the Church.

Questions for Application

40 minutes
Choose questions according to your interest and time.

1 John introduces images of the devil, but only in the context of new images of Jesus' death, resurrection, and authority. What might be the significance of this context?

2 Christians who participated in emperor worship were joining in something socially acceptable but incompatible with faithfulness to Jesus. How can we become aware of our own blind spots to attitudes and behavior that are socially accepted but are contrary to our call to discipleship?

3 When have you realized that you needed to make a break with some widely accepted practice or value out of faithfulness to Jesus?

4 What should Christians do when they feel guilty?

5 Chapter 12 twice mentions "testimony" to Jesus. In what way do you bear witness to Jesus? How might God be calling you to do this more or differently?

When the discussion raises difficulties, "group members can volunteer to research questions to get additional information from other sources."

Loretta Girzaitis, *Guidebook for Bible Study*

Approach to Prayer

15 minutes
Use this approach—or create your own!

✦ The reading portrays the devil as a deceiver seeking to destroy the Church through falsehood (12:15). Give everyone a few minutes for silent reflection on these questions: What is an area of life where you experience temptation? Who are the tempters and deceivers in your life? How do you intend to confront them? Invite participants to share their reflections, if they wish, and to offer brief prayers for one another. Then pray this prayer:

St. Michael the archangel, defend us in battle. Be our protection against the wickedness and snares of the devil. May God rebuke him, we humbly pray, and may you, prince of the heavenly armies, by the power of God thrust into hell Satan and all the evil spirits that roam through the world seeking the ruin of souls. Amen.

To conclude, pray a Hail Mary and an Our Father.

A Living Tradition

A Woman Clothed with the Sun

This section is a supplement for individual reading.

The woman in Revelation 12 is surely one of the most splendid and intriguing images to appear in John's visions. "Clothed with the sun, with the moon under her feet, and on her head a crown of twelve stars," she radiates the brightness of heaven (12:1). Yet she is earthly and vulnerable also. She shouts in pain as her child is born; she is chased into the wilderness by a dragon.

With her heavenly majesty and her earthly suffering, the woman symbolizes the people of God. In the first scene, she represents the people of Israel up to the coming of the Messiah, for the Messiah comes from God's people (12:1–6). In the second scene, she represents the Church, confronted with temptations and deceptions yet always protected by God (12:13–17).

John's vision especially emphasizes the more-than-earthly mystery of the Church. As scholar Gregory Beale writes, "The woman's brightness connotes the heavenly identity and heavenly protection of the people of God, as well as their purity, which safeguards their ultimate spiritual invincibility against persecution and corruption by temptation, deception, or any vice."

When we read about the symbolic woman who gives birth to the Messiah, we cannot help but think of the woman of Nazareth who really did bear the Messiah. Mary appears in the Gospels as an ordinary, earthly person without heavenly splendor. Yet she is heavenly in the way that it is possible on earth. She received God's word with attention. She responded to God's plan with trust and wholehearted cooperation. She was overshadowed by the Spirit. Christians recognize in her a perfection flowing from a purity safeguarded from the moment of her conception. They believe that God gave her invincibility against corruption by assuming her into heaven after her death.

Christians, then, see Mary as the model of the Church—an example of earthly life fully transformed by God's grace and made radiant with the light of heaven. Thus the woman of Revelation 12 and the woman of the Gospels converge. As a symbol of the people of God, the woman clothed with the sun is also a symbol of Mary, for Mary herself is the perfect representation of God's people.

Between Discussions

In the next chapters, John's visions range widely in time and space. More beasts appear (chapter 13). There is praise of the Lamb, final judgment, and more praise (chapters 14–15). After another series of seven (chapter 16), we meet a prostitute who symbolizes an evil city (chapters 17–18). Obviously Revelation does not have a simple structure! For centuries, scholars have attempted to discern John's outline. Considering its complexity, historian Leonard L. Thompson may be right when he says that Revelation does not *have* an outline but can best be envisioned as a stream flowing in and out of various images, creating whorls and eddies as it goes.

To return to chapter 13, the newly arrived beasts have almost a cartoonlike quality, although they represent deadly evil. They reminded John's first readers of the worship of the Roman emperors. The cities of Asia led the trend in giving the emperors divine honors. All the cities where John's readers lived had shrines or altars for the emperors. The province of Asia even changed its calendar to make the emperor Augustus's birthday New Year's Day. On that day the cities were filled with processions. Residents were expected to offer incense on mini-altars in front of their houses as the crowds paraded by. Special priests conducted worship before statues of the emperors—a practice reflected in the third monster's orchestration of worship before the image, probably a statue, of the second monster (13:14–15).

Ominously, the second beast initiates a fierce persecution of everyone who will not worship the image (13:14–15). This expresses John's prophetic sense that pressures on Christians to participate in emperor worship are about to intensify. Shortly before John wrote his letter, the city of Ephesus erected a splendid temple to the imperial family, containing a twenty-foot-high statue of the emperor as a god. To mark its completion the city held a sort of Olympic Games, constructing for the purpose an enormous, permanent sports complex more than three football fields long— with the emperor's name all over it, of course. Built right at the center of town, without regard to expense or other interests, the gigantic sports facility announced to everyone who walked through

Ephesus, *"No one* is more important to us than the emperor." Such developments must have strengthened John's foreboding that Christians were headed for a showdown with the government.

Other aspects of the beasts also allude to the Roman emperors. Scholars detect an echo of a legend about the emperor Nero in the description of the first beast's mortal wound that healed (13:3). But John is not writing in code to provide insider information about political developments. He is using symbols to help his readers grasp the true nature of the situation they face. So, for example, John employs the Nero legend not to speak about Nero but to show a similarity between Jesus and the "divine" emperor. Both appear to have died yet are alive again, bearing the mark of the death wound (1:18; 5:6; 13:3). Both claim to have a life force even greater than death and, therefore, to be a source of life for others. Obviously only one can be the real source of life, and —this is John's point—people must choose one or the other.

Quite likely the famous "number of the beast" (13:18) is also a symbol rather than a cipher (just as the number in the next verse is symbolic). There have been interminable efforts to connect 666 with a particular emperor. But John's purpose is probably to symbolize the nature of the evil at work in emperor worship. Since *seven* represents completeness, *six* represents incompleteness. In effect, John's symbolic number means that the emperor is absolutely incomplete. No matter how powerful, no human being, not even the Roman emperor, can attain the status of God and become a source of life for others.

In image after image, a series of contrasts reinforces John's message that Christians must choose between the Roman emperor, acclaimed as the great benefactor and the source of peace and prosperity, and Jesus, true emperor of the universe and benefactor of the human race. What is the message in this for us? We do not confront emperor worship, but we do face the temptation to regard other powers as crucial for our lives. We too must choose where to place our basic trust.

LOOK, A WHITE HORSE!

Questions to Begin

15 minutes
Use a question or two to get warmed up for the reading.

---

1 From movies you've seen or books you've read, what's your favorite showdown (fictional or real-life) between good and evil? What made it satisfying? Do you always like to see the good guys win?

---

2 Who is your favorite Christian martyr? Why? Make a list of participants' favorites, and hold on to it for the prayer time.

Opening the Bible

5 minutes
Have someone in the group read "The Reading" aloud. (If participants have not already read "What's Happened," read that aloud also. Otherwise skip it.)

What's Happened

In a rapidly changing series of visions, John sees the two beasts persecute all people who identify themselves with the Lamb (chapter 13), final judgment (14:14–20), more symbolic disasters (chapter 16), and the appearance and destruction of a vast system of social evil represented by a "great whore" (17:1–19:10).

The Reading: Revelation 19:11–20:10

Final Judgment

11 Then I saw heaven opened, and there was a white horse! Its rider is called Faithful and True, and in righteousness he judges and makes war. 12 His eyes are like a flame of fire, and on his head are many diadems; and he has a name inscribed that no one knows but himself. 13 He is clothed in a robe dipped in blood, and his name is called The Word of God. 14 And the armies of heaven, wearing fine linen, white and pure, were following him on white horses. 15 From his mouth comes a sharp sword with which to strike down the nations, and he will rule them with a rod of iron; he will tread the wine press of the fury of the wrath of God the Almighty. 16 On his robe and on his thigh he has a name inscribed, "King of kings and Lord of lords."

The Forces of Evil Are Destroyed

17 Then I saw an angel standing in the sun, and with a loud voice he called to all the birds that fly in midheaven, "Come, gather for the great supper of God, 18 to eat the flesh of kings, the flesh of captains, the flesh of the mighty, the flesh of horses and their riders—flesh of all, both free and slave, both small and great." 19 Then I saw the beast and the kings of the earth with their armies gathered to make war against the rider on the horse and against his army. 20 And the beast was captured, and with it the false prophet who had performed in its presence the signs by which he deceived those who had received the mark of the beast and those who worshiped its image. These two were thrown alive into the lake of fire that burns with sulfur. 21 And the rest were killed by the sword of the rider on the horse, the sword

that came from his mouth; and all the birds were gorged with their flesh.

A Thousand-Year Reign

20:1 Then I saw an angel coming down from heaven, holding in his hand the key to the bottomless pit and a great chain. 2 He seized the dragon, that ancient serpent, who is the Devil and Satan, and bound him for a thousand years, 3 and threw him into the pit, and locked and sealed it over him, so that he would deceive the nations no more, until the thousand years were ended. After that he must be let out for a little while.

4 Then I saw thrones, and those seated on them were given authority to judge. I also saw the souls of those who had been beheaded for their testimony to Jesus and for the word of God. They had not worshiped the beast or its image and had not received its mark on their foreheads or their hands. They came to life and reigned with Christ a thousand years. 5 (The rest of the dead did not come to life until the thousand years were ended.) This is the first resurrection. 6 Blessed and holy are those who share in the first resurrection. Over these the second death has no power, but they will be priests of God and of Christ, and they will reign with him a thousand years.

7 When the thousand years are ended, Satan will be released from his prison 8 and will come out to deceive the nations at the four corners of the earth, Gog and Magog, in order to gather them for battle; they are as numerous as the sands of the sea. 9 They marched up over the breadth of the earth and surrounded the camp of the saints and the beloved city. And fire came down from heaven and consumed them. 10 And the devil who had deceived them was thrown into the lake of fire and sulfur, where the beast and the false prophet were, and they will be tormented day and night forever and ever.

Questions for Careful Reading

10 minutes
Choose questions according to your interest and time.

1 The main image of Jesus in Revelation is the Lamb. What does the imagery of 19:11–21 add to the total picture of Jesus? How can the two images of Jesus be combined?

2 What is the similarity between those who ride with Jesus in 19:14 and those pictured in 6:11 and 7:9? What does this similarity suggest about the identity of the cavalry in 19:14?

3 In 19:11 John indicates that 19:11–21 symbolizes a judgment ("he judges"). Compare this vision to other visions of God's judgment in 6:12–17 and 20:11–15. What different aspects of God's judgment does each vision emphasize?

4 In 20:3 John says that the dragon was prevented from deceiving. What does 20:8 tell us about the purpose of the dragon's deception? John does not explicitly state the lie that the dragon was promoting. Judging from 20:8, what would you guess it was? (There is no one correct answer.)

65

A Guide to the Reading

If participants have not read this section already, read it aloud.
Otherwise go on to "Questions for Application."

John presents a vision of final judgment and the end of the world (19:11–21), as he did in a selection we read earlier (6:12–17), and it is instructive to compare the two passages. The visions are very different. If John had intended to tell us what the end of the world will actually look like, he would hardly have given us such different accounts. The differences remind us he is showing the inner dynamics and meanings of events, not providing journalistic descriptions. Similarly, Jesus offered various parables to convey what the kingdom of God is all about, although none describes what the kingdom actually looks like.

The symbolic nature of John's vision is important to keep in mind, for while the imagery of the rider on the white horse belongs to the battlefield, the meaning belongs to the courtroom. John has taken the metaphor of legal battle and developed it into an impressive, if gruesome, picture. Jesus spoke of the final judgment in shepherding terms (Matthew 25:31–32); John expresses it here in terms of war. The warrior is essentially a judge (19:11). He has the penetrating vision needed to adjudicate all cases fairly (19:12). His only weapon—indeed, the only weapon in his entire army—is his sword, which is the word coming from his mouth (19:15).

Earlier John presented Jesus as the "faithful and true witness" to God's love in the world who summed up his testimony on the cross (3:14). Now John shows Jesus at the end of time, still "Faithful and True" (19:11), bearing the same testimony to God's love that he gave at Calvary. Jesus' faithfulness and truth now bring a verdict of guilty against the world's evil. How can this be?

The cross stands as the supreme expression of God's mercy. At the same time, it exposes the nature of human society alienated from God. The crucifixion of Jesus shows what sinful human beings think of God's mercy and faithfulness: we find it gets in the way of our plans; it is troublesome, even dangerous, an object of hatred and contempt. The crucifixion is damning evidence of the underlying evil at work in a human society that rejects God— evidence that secures the world's conviction in the court of final judgment. John does not give us any notion of how this conviction will actually take place, but he reveals the factor on which judgment will hinge: our response to Jesus' cross. Have we accepted or rejected the mercy of God that Jesus, the faithful and true one, bore witness to on the cross? Have we taken up our cross and followed Jesus?

The bloodstains on Jesus' robe (19:13) are likely a sign of his followers' martyrdom. Their faithful witness to God's love also appears in evidence at the final judgment against those who have rejected God's love.

The annihilation of the evil army (19:17–21) symbolizes God's absolute destruction of the systems of evil in the world. They no longer have any power to harm. No wish is expressed that any particular people be sent to hell. We can desire the complete end of a genocidal regime while hoping its leaders find forgiveness.

"Then" comes a thousand-year period (20:1–10). But what does *then* mean here? John's visions shuttle back and forth between past, present, and future. Quite likely *then* does not mean that the thousand years followed the judgment in chapter 19 chronologically. Rather, after seeing the vision in chapter 19, John saw another vision. Like the visions in chapters 5 and 12, this one takes us back once more to Jesus' resurrection.

Many people suppose the thousand-year reign of Christ and the saints will be an earthly kingdom. Significantly, John does not say the thrones are on earth. They are probably in heaven, like all the other thrones in Revelation except for the dragon's (13:2). Ever since his resurrection, Jesus has reigned over the earth, but it is not and never will be an earthly, political reign. The devil is restrained to some extent, unable to marshal his forces for a final confrontation with God (20:3, 7–8). But many New Testament passages speak of the devil's being curtailed without meaning he is rendered inoperative (Matthew 12:29; Luke 10:17–20; John 12:31–33; Colossians 2:15; 2 Thessalonians 2:6–12; Hebrews 2:14). The present reign of Jesus remains a time of spiritual conflict.

The enthroned ones are those who have died faithful to Jesus (20:4). They are already alive with him, sharing like royalty in his victory over death, serving as priests in God's presence.

Questions for Application

40 minutes
Choose questions according to your interest and time.

1 What makes it difficult to oppose injustice or wrongdoing, either social or individual, while loving the people involved? How can we overcome the difficulties?

2 What message of hope does 19:11–21 convey? What difference can this message make in your life?

3 What do the titles of Jesus in 19:11, 13, and 16 mean for your relationship with him?

4   Describe a situation in which God's Word had an effect on you. What did you learn?

5   How is God inviting you to respond to his mercy and love at this point in your life?

6   Does it come as a surprise to think that you are already living during the thousand-year reign of Christ? What signs of his reign do you see? How should this perspective affect the way you live today?

"We are not to waste time with subtleties and fruitless discussions. The important question is: 'What has this passage to tell us about our Christian life?'"

James Rauner, *The Young Church in Action*

Approach to Prayer

15 minutes
Use this approach—or create your own!

✦ Give participants an opportunity to share about one area of life where they feel God is calling them to stand firm or make a change—and about what makes it difficult to respond. Then offer spontaneous prayers for each other, asking for God's help. If you identified favorite martyrs at the beginning of your discussion (page 62), continue with prayers to those martyrs in the form of "[Martyr's name], pray for us." End with the Our Father.

Saints in the Making

Sometimes Love Speaks Harshly

This section is a supplement for individual reading.

Even though we know John's visions are symbolic, the savage conflict in chapter 19 may give us the impression that his attitude is vengeful. To grasp the message of love in John's language of conflict, it is helpful to listen to other Christians who have faced persecution.

A modern example is a Lithuanian named Nijole Sadunaite. Soviet authorities tried her in 1975 for publishing a report on Soviet religious repression. At her trial Sadunaite told the prosecutor and judges, "I love you all as if you were my brothers and sisters, and I would not hesitate to give my life for each of you." However, she said, they did not need her sacrifice; they needed a dose of truth about their totalitarian system, which "infringes the most elementary of human rights." Citing the maxim "Only he who loves has the right to reprimand," she warned the government representatives that "every day your crimes are bringing you closer to the dust-heap of history"—an image of destruction John would have relished.

Like John, Sadunaite spoke in terms of struggle and conquest, yet conquest not by force but by love. "Not only have I fought for human rights and justice, but I'm being punished for doing so. My sentence will be my triumph!" she declared. "I will gladly lose my freedom for the freedom of others, and I'm willing to die so that others may live."

John would have nodded in agreement when Sadunaite said, "We have to condemn evil as harshly as possible, but we must love men, even if they are wrong." She added, "We can learn to do this in the school of Jesus Christ." The image of learning in the Lamb's classroom is reminiscent of John's image of washing our clothes in the Lamb's blood.

Sadunaite spent several years in a concentration camp and exile in Siberia. British scholar Michael Bourdeaux wrote, "The most impressive aspect of her letters is the complete lack of self-pity and the spiritual security they express; in almost every letter she thanks God for his goodness to her and rejoices at the beauty of the Siberian landscape and the friendliness of her fellow workers."

Between Discussions

Many of John's visions in chapters 6–20 have symbolically represented history from Jesus' resurrection to his return. The horsemen who rode forth at the breaking of the seals (6:1–8) showed us God bending even the worst human evils, such as war and economic oppression, to serve his purposes. The vision we have just seen of the thousand-year reign (20:1–6) showed that throughout history those who die in union with Jesus already share his conquest of death.

John has repeatedly run up to the end of history and the final judgment, always backing off from describing what lies beyond. He has presented images of the judgment by which God will bring history to a conclusion (6:12–17; 19:11–21), but each time he has returned to view history from yet another angle.

Now, however, John has reached the end of his visions of history. He portrays the final judgment one last time (20:11–15). From this point on, rather than returning to history, he breaks through into the new creation that lies beyond time and space (chapters 21–22).

The outstanding feature of John's final vision of the judgment is the great white throne (20:11)—the first thing he saw in heaven (4:2). G. B. Caird remarks, "From first to last John's vision is dominated by this symbol of divine sovereignty. The final reality which will still be standing when heaven and earth have disappeared is the great white throne." The Enthroned One, with the Lamb, was before anything was, he is now, and he will be when all things have passed away (1:8, 17; 4:8). John's visions give us a conception of God as beginning and center and end of all. Reading Revelation is an opportunity for us to reshape our view of reality.

Earlier visions looked at the judgment from various angles. One vision symbolized the way sin affects our perception of God (6:12–17): those who fled in terror from God experienced him as wrathful rather than merciful because they had stubbornly refused to repent of their sins. Other visions portrayed what we might call the group dimension of judgment: the army of rebellion was defeated, and the monstrous ringleaders were thrown into a fiery lake (19:20; 20:10). Such corporate images symbolized God's inevitable destruction of systems of evil. Perhaps, if John were writing today, he would make this point by describing cartoonlike animals with names like Consumerism and Racism and Abortion being herded up a ramp into a slaughterhouse.

In contrast, John's final vision of judgment accents the importance of our individual response to God (20:11–15). The pivotal statement lies in verse 13, where the Greek literally speaks of *each* person facing God's judgment. The old Catholic translation rendered it precisely: "They were judged, every *one* according to their works." Out of the mass of humanity standing in court, each of us will step forward and approach the bench individually, while the clerk opens the directory of human affairs to our particular page.

Knowing the account of our selfishness and sin recorded there, each of us might expect to hear a verdict of guilty. But beside the book of our deeds is another, the book of life (20:12, 15). This is the book of the Lamb (13:8; 21:27). Those whose names are written in the Lamb's book are those who were earlier described as having washed their clothing in the Lamb's blood. Gregory Beale writes, "They do not suffer judgment for their evil deeds because he has already suffered it for them. . . . The 'book' is metaphorical for God's unfailing memory, and at the end God recognizes those who have taken refuge in the Lamb."

The final judgment brings the drama of human history to a close. Old heaven and earth pass away, and God creates anew (21:1–8). In the new creation there is no sea (21:1)—a way of saying there is no source of rebellion against God (compare 13:1).

God is not *part* of this new creation; he is its central reality. As M. Eugene Boring writes, "At the End we meet not an event but a Person. . . . In 21:3 a voice interprets the descending city as 'God's dwelling with humanity.' . . . God does not merely bring the End, God *is* the End."

A City Coming Down from Heaven

Questions to Begin

15 minutes
Use a question or two to get warmed up for the reading.

---

1 What is your birthstone? favorite
jewel? Have you ever seen royal
jewels on display
at a museum or in a television
program? What is the attraction
of jewels, pearls, gold?

---

2 If you had the power to create
the ideal community—the place
of your dreams where you would
like to live forever—what would
it be like? Who would be there?
How would it be different from
where you live now?

---

3 Why do people sometimes
use feminine pronouns when
referring to cities and ships?

5 minutes
Have someone in the group read "The Reading" aloud. (If participants have not already read "What's Happened," read that aloud also. Otherwise skip it.)

What's Happened

The last reading portrayed the final defeat of Satan. A vision of final judgment followed (20:11–15). Chapter 21 begins with a buildup to visions of the heavenly city. God announces that he has completed everything he intended to accomplish (21:6). Now a new creation comes into view—a symbolic representation of the life of perfect, uninterrupted unity with God that human beings are destined to enjoy.

The Reading: Revelation 21:9–22:5

Admiring the Skyline

9 Then one of the seven angels . . . came and said to me, "Come, I will show you the bride, the wife of the Lamb." 10 And in the spirit he carried me away to a great, high mountain and showed me the holy city Jerusalem coming down out of heaven from God. 11 It has the glory of God and a radiance like a very rare jewel, like jasper, clear as crystal. 12 It has a great, high wall with twelve gates, and at the gates twelve angels, and on the gates are inscribed the names of the twelve tribes of the Israelites; 13 on the east three gates, on the north three gates, on the south three gates, and on the west three gates. 14 And the wall of the city has twelve foundations, and on them are the twelve names of the twelve apostles of the Lamb.

15 The angel who talked to me had a measuring rod of gold to measure the city and its gates and walls. 16 The city lies foursquare, its length the same as its width; and he measured the city with his rod, fifteen hundred miles;* its length and width and height are equal. 17 He also measured its wall, one hundred forty-four cubits by human measurement, which the angel was using. 18 The wall is built of jasper, while the city is pure gold, clear as glass. 19 The foundations of the

* The Greek literally says that the city is the length and width of twelve thousand sports stadiums (notice the repeated use of *twelve*).

wall of the city are adorned with every jewel; the first was jasper. . . .
²¹ And the twelve gates are twelve pearls, each of the gates is a single
pearl, and the street of the city is pure gold, transparent as glass.

Exploring the Main Plaza

²² I saw no temple in the city, for its temple is the Lord God the
Almighty and the Lamb. ²³ And the city has no need of sun or moon
to shine on it, for the glory of God is its light, and its lamp is the
Lamb. ²⁴ The nations will walk by its light, and the kings of the earth
will bring their glory into it. ²⁵ Its gates will never be shut by day—
and there will be no night there. ²⁶ People will bring into it the glory
and the honor of the nations. ²⁷ But nothing unclean will enter it, nor
anyone who practices abomination or falsehood, but only those who
are written in the Lamb's book of life.

    ²²:¹ Then the angel showed me the river of the water of life,
bright as crystal, flowing from the throne of God and of the Lamb
² through the middle of the street of the city. On either side of the
river is the tree of life with its twelve kinds of fruit, producing its fruit
each month; and the leaves of the tree are for the healing of the nations.
³ Nothing accursed will be found there any more. But the throne of
God and of the Lamb will be in it, and his servants will worship him;
⁴ they will see his face, and his name will be on their foreheads. ⁵ And
there will be no more night; they need no light of lamp or sun, for the
Lord God will be their light, and they will reign forever and ever.

10 minutes
Choose questions according to your interest and time.

1 There are no nights in the city, but there are days and months (21:25; 22:2). What does this inconsistency suggest about the kind of picture John is presenting?

2 What similarities are there between the heavenly Jerusalem here and the description of heaven in chapters 4 and 5? What might be the significance of these similarities?

3 How many references to light and brightness can you find? What total impression of the city do these create? What do you think is the significance of this aspect of the city?

4 What do the features of the city suggest about how people who wish to live in the city should conduct their lives in the present world?

5 Apart from any particular details, what does John's symbolic vision of a city suggest about eternal life with God?

A Guide to the Reading

If participants have not read this section already, read it aloud. Otherwise go on to "Questions for Application."

Journey's end. After passing for long ages through "this valley of tears"—as an old prayer regards the world—humanity emerges into light and splendor. The human race comes home to God. John's visions have shed light on God's activity through the Lamb in a world that often rejects him and claims godlike powers for itself. John's final visions illuminate the final outcome toward which God is working.

As on earlier occasions, John hears one thing and sees another (compare 5:5–6; 7:4, 9). An angel tells John he will show him the bride of the Lamb; John sees a city. Obviously the bride and the city are both symbols—one speaking of our joy and intimacy with God, the other speaking of our community with one another. When it comes to communicating about eternal life with God, symbols are as much as we can handle. The actual nature of our final state is as far beyond our capacity to comprehend as computers are beyond the understanding of my dog. John's vision stirs our hearts without satisfying our curiosity.

The city appears in two pictures—one viewing it from the outside, the other from the inside. Essentially both make the same point: at the end of all things, God will be with his people.

In the first view (21:10–21) the city appears as an immense cube, literally *twelve* thousand stadiums long. As always, the number twelve refers to the twelve tribes, that is, the whole people of Israel. The city's immensity—it is fifteen hundred miles on a side—indicates it will be the residence of the entire redeemed human race. All will finally dwell together in one society. The squareness of the city indicates its perfection. The shape also alludes to the inner chamber of the Jerusalem temple; the holy of holies, where God made himself extraordinarily present, was likewise a cube (1 Kings 6:20). Only the high priest entered the holy of holies. In contrast, Gregory Beale writes, "The whole community of the redeemed is considered priests serving in the temple and privileged to see God's face in the new holy of holies, which now encompasses the entire temple-city."

If the city as a whole is a temple, it is also a throne. In John's first heavenly vision, God appeared as a blaze of jasper green light above the great white throne (4:3). Now the entire heavenly city is suffused with "a radiance like a very rare jewel, like jasper" (21:11; see also 21:18–20). God will be with his people as a king sitting on his throne. What better image could there be for God's total, immediate life-giving reign over us?

The measuring of the city and its "great, high wall" (21:12, 15–17) is a way of certifying the absolute safety that God's people will enjoy. Nothing inside or outside ourselves will any longer jeopardize our enjoyment of God's presence.

Like the first picture of the city, the second (21:22–22:5) shows that the entire city is the temple of God's presence (21:22) and the throne room where he rules (22:3–5). The second picture also indicates that all evil has been removed. There are no longer any liars to distort the truth about God (21:27; 22:3). No sin or deception any longer separates the peoples of the world from God, and they come on pilgrimage with offerings for God (21:24). The heavenly city is not a gated community; its gates need never be closed because the city has no enemies. Its residents are completely secure (21:25).

The second picture is less interested in surveying the city's perimeter than in exploring what lies within. Inside the city John is struck by the radiance that shines everywhere (21:23; 22:5), a radiance that is the light of God himself. John also sees a river, a throne, a street, and a tree (22:1–2). The arrangement of these features is not entirely clear, but it seems John wishes to emphasize that the tree lies at the *center* of the city. Its location indicates its identity, for this is the same life-giving tree that stood in the *middle* of the garden of Eden (Genesis 3:3). It was sealed off from human beings when they began to sin (Genesis 3:22–24). The tree now stands unfenced in the main square of the city, accessible to all. Jesus has restored to us the eternal life for which we were created.

Questions for Application

40 minutes
Choose questions according to your interest and time.

1 John's vision of the heavenly Jerusalem symbolizes God's desire for you to know him and be with him completely. How much do you desire that? How much do you think about it? What other desires in your life compete with that one?

2 What step could you take to respond to God's invitation to love him more deeply?

3 How would it change the way you relate to the people in your daily life if you viewed them as potential future fellow citizens in the heavenly Jerusalem? What can you do to help other people take the place that God has prepared for them?

4 How could you bring your community—family, city, parish, associations—more in line with the final vision of human life that John shows us in this reading?

5 What is the most important message that you will take from your reading of Revelation? What response will you make to God's Word?

"The Holy Spirit, who inspired the writers of the Bible, guides both the present discussion and the lives of the group members."

John Burke, O.P., *Beginners' Guide to Bible Sharing*

Approach to Prayer

15 minutes
Use this approach—or create your own!

✦ Have one person read Revelation 21:22–22:5 aloud, pausing between sentences. Allow a few minutes for silent reflection. Then let another participant read Revelation 22:12–21 in the same way.

Give an opportunity for participants to pray spontaneously.

End with an Our Father.

A Living Tradition

God Himself Is Their House

This section is a supplement for individual reading.

Bede, an English monk who lived in the eighth century, wrote a commentary on Revelation that was popular for a long time. Here is a sample of his comments on John's vision of the heavenly Jerusalem:

21:16 "Its length and width and height are equal." This is the solidity of the unconquerable truth by which the Church, supported by the length of faith, the breadth of love, and the height of hope, cannot be shifted from its foundations by any wind of false teaching (see Ephesians 3:16–19; 4:14).

21:22 "I saw no temple in the city." Although, John says, I declared that the city is built with stones, I did not mean that the saints rest in a material building, for God himself is their house and light and rest.

21:23 "The glory of God is its light." In our home country, heaven, we will enjoy the very same light that now rules us as we walk along the road of life. By that light we now are able to distinguish between good and evil; then by that light, completely happy, we will see only good things.

21:25 "Its gates will never be shut by day." This is a sign of absolute security, for there it will no longer be said, "Stay awake and pray that you may not come into the time of trial" (Matthew 26:41) but rather, "Be still, and know that I am God!" (Psalm 46:10).

21:27 "Nothing unclean will enter it." No unclean person or liar will see the light of the city that he hated, because darkness will have blinded his eyes.

22:1 "The angel showed me the river of the water of life." This is not a representation of the celebration of baptism but rather a revelation of the outcome of that sacrament. Now the Church sows in the Spirit, so that then in the Spirit it may reap eternal life (see Galatians 6:7–9).

22:2 "On either side of the river is the tree of life." This tree of life you may interpret either as the glory of the holy cross or as the Lord Christ.

After Words

If you compare the end of Revelation to its beginning (compare 22:6–21 to 1:1–8), you will immediately notice similarities. John began by describing his letter as God's revelation, showing his servants what must happen soon; this affirmation is repeated at the close (1:1; 22:6). Both the introduction and the afterword declare that the person who keeps the words of the prophecy will be blessed (1:3; 22:7). In various ways, the opening and closing verses form a frame around the body of the letter. Indeed, these sections show that the writing is a letter, for they contain the normal expressions for opening and closing a Greek letter (1:4; 22:21).

On further examination, you may also notice a similarity between the section that follows the opening (chapters 2–3) and the section that precedes the closing (21:9–22:5). Both sections concern the Church. The earlier section consists of letters to seven local church communities; the later section presents a vision of the Church to come. It seems that John has deliberately structured his letter this way in order to lead his readers to reflect on the relationship between how they are at present and how God ultimately intends them to be.

There is a striking contrast between the present condition of the seven churches and the final condition they are to share in the new creation. Judging from Jesus' assessments of them, we know that the seven church communities are struggling—not entirely successfully, perhaps not even very hard—to remain faithful to Jesus. Many members are making fundamental compromises with the pagan culture in order to avoid economic or political sanctions. The future Church will be thoroughly united to Jesus, completely filled with his light and life.

By setting the picture of the present, imperfect churches next to the picture of the future, perfect Church, John prods his readers to reflect on their destiny as God's people. John would like them to realize that underneath their wavering and worldliness, their true nature is a community totally identified with Jesus. Their destiny is to be transfigured by his radiance. Gregory Beale writes that John presents the vision of the perfected Church "to exhort the faithful community of the present to begin to reflect the facets of their coming consummated excellence." They should start acting like the people they are ultimately going to be: a community of people completely in love with Jesus and with one another.

The vision of the new Jerusalem does not satisfy our curiosity about the exact nature of our future risen life, but it shows us enough for us to grasp that it is a gift beyond compare. As another scholar, M. Eugene Boring, puts it, "The gift becomes an assignment." When we perceive the gift of life that God intends for us, we can see how we ought to live here and now. Boring writes, "If this is where the world is going, then every thought, move, deed in some other direction is out of step with reality and is finally wasted. The picture does not attempt to answer speculative questions about the future; it is offered as an orientation for life in the present." Or, as Kathleen Norris writes, "It asks us to believe that only the good remains, at the end, and directs us toward carefully tending it here and now."

This, of course, is the purpose of John's whole letter. The central section of the letter—between the two visions of the great white throne (4:2; 20:11)—opens our eyes to the present reality of Jesus' rule over human history. John has shown us the paradoxical way that Jesus has entered into his kingship—through death on a cross. He has shown us Jesus' mastery over the forces of evil, which he harnesses to serve his redeeming purposes. He has shown us the ugliness and futility of all the injustice and sin in the world. He has shown us the way we can share in Jesus' conquest of sin and death —by joining him in his faithful testimony to God's love, even to the point of death.

The first recipients of John's letter read it aloud when they gathered to celebrate the Eucharist. When they reached the end, they rolled up the scroll and placed bread and wine on a table. Their leader prayed a eucharistic prayer, and they entered into the mysteries they had just heard John describe. Standing before the throne of God, surrounded by the heavenly beings, they praised and thanked him for the death and resurrection of his Son. The Lamb became present to them, and they feasted on him as the manna for their exodus journey. Celebrating the Eucharist, they tasted the life that lies beyond this one. And so do we.

W hat's wrong with saying, 'Lord Caesar!' and burning incense, and doing other such things in order to save yourself?"

Asking the question was the chief of police in the city of Smyrna. He was having a conversation with Polycarp, the elderly local bishop. Polycarp had been arrested, and the two men were sitting in a carriage parked outside the civic stadium, where a blood-thirsty crowd was hoping to watch Polycarp die a grisly death. It was about the year 155, some sixty-five years after John wrote to Christians in Smyrna and its neighboring cities (2:8–11).

In response to the question, Polycarp made it clear he had no intention of avoiding death by offering token acknowledgment to the "divine" emperor. This seeming unreasonableness so enraged the police chief that he literally threw Polycarp out of his carriage.

While admiring Polycarp's courage, we may ask the same question the police chief put to him. What *was* the harm in saying a few reverent words about the emperor and offering a pinch of incense? Why were Polycarp and other early Christians, such as John, adamant in their refusal to participate in emperor worship and other aspects of pagan religion? And what significance does their example have for us today?

Christians in the Roman Empire inherited the tradition of Israel, which, in the most uncompromising terms, condemned treating anyone or anything as God except the one God of Israel. Other religions, which had numerous gods, could accommodate additional deities. The God of Israel was unique in his insistence on his unique-ness. "I am the LORD your God," he declared in the first of the Ten Commandments. "You shall have no other gods before me . . . for I the LORD your God am a jealous God" (Exodus 20:2–5).

God demanded undiluted loyalty because he cared about how his people lived. Choosing a deity means choosing more than which shrine you worship at. Religion shapes how you see yourself and the world, your view of why you are alive and what you should do with your life. Other religions were different in crucial respects from the worship of the God of Israel. Whenever the Israelites began to make a place for pagan gods alongside the God of Israel, their values and practices inevitably shifted. The wealthy felt less restrained from preying on the poor (1 Kings 16:29–33; 21:1–16). Sexual immorality increased (Jeremiah 2:20–24).

We are changed by the God or god to whom we submit. Materially, we are what we eat. Spiritually, we become who we worship. Worship the God of Israel and you will begin to reflect his character: faithfulness, trustworthiness, kindness to the needy, willingness to forgive. Worship other gods and you will take on their characteristics instead.

A deeper reason for the Israelites not to dabble in paganism lay in God's desire for a personal relationship with them. God saw Israel as his bride (Hosea 2). That is a powerful image, for marriage is the most intimate, most exclusive human relationship. A consumer may shop at many stores; a patient may seek treatment from many doctors. But a husband may not caress any other women, and a wife may not flirt with any other men, for to do so strikes at the heart of their marriage. Quite simply, God wanted his people's love. "I the Lord your God am a jealous God."

Like the leaders of Israel before Jesus' time, John grasped these reasons for utterly avoiding involvement with pagan religions. John was deeply concerned about the selfish materialism of his society, which was fostered by pagan religious practices. In John's view, to participate in pagan religious practices was to buy into the value system and lifestyle that went with them.

The connections between pagan religion and worldly values are represented in Revelation by a symbol that even John finds shocking (17:6). John sees an expensively clad prostitute sitting on a monster that represents pagan emperor worship and offering her clients an intoxicating drink (17:1–4). She represents the social system confronting John's readers—its paganism, its oppressive political power, its morally corrupting wealth. In particular, she symbolizes the all-consuming pursuit of a comfortable and prestigious lifestyle. When she is destroyed, merchants bemoan her demise, remembering her fine foods, fashionable apparel, and other consumer goods (18:11–17). John wishes his Christian friends to look at the "great whore" and realize that here is evil which must be avoided at all costs.

John shows what happens to Christians who compromise with the linked evils of paganism and materialism. They end up like the Christian community in Laodicea, one of the seven communities to which the letter is addressed (1:11). The Christians in Laodicea were compromisers (3:14–22). They accommodated themselves to the pagan culture of Laodicea, symbolized by the stream of undrinkable lukewarm water that flowed through their city (3:15–16). They were probably taking part in the idolatrous practices woven into the fabric of business and civic life in Laodicea (compare 2:14) and sharing in the materialistic outlook bound up with pagan religion. Quite possibly they were keeping quiet about their belief in Jesus.

This approach brought them prosperity, but in the process they lost sight of their need for God. They became blind to their sins (3:17–20). Far from being meaningless, the words of honor they offered to the emperor and the incense they burned to pagan gods signified their adoption of a lifestyle at odds with Jesus and the gospel.

Christians appear in John's visions as male virgins (14:4). This is a symbolic way of showing that all Christians, men and women, married and single, are to preserve a single-hearted love for Jesus in expectation of being fully united to him. With even clearer nuptial symbolism, the whole Church appears as a bride (21:2). These images underline the exclusive bond of love Jesus wishes to have with his followers. By implication, any participation in paganism is an unfaithful dalliance, a kind of adultery.

This was the ultimate reason Bishop Polycarp gave for declining to save himself from execution by making a small gesture of emperor worship. After being thrown out of the police chief's carriage, he was escorted into the stadium and brought before the proconsul, the highest Roman official in the region. The proconsul made one last attempt to persuade him, in light of his advanced age, to save himself. "Swear by Caesar and say something insulting about Christ, and I will let you go," he urged. Polycarp replied, "For eighty-six years I have served Jesus, and never once did he do me any wrong. How could I say anything against my king, who saved me?" When further appeals proved futile, the proconsul had Polycarp tied to a stake in the middle of the stadium. To the immense satisfaction of the crowd, Polycarp was burned to death.

Almost two millennia after John and Polycarp, our situation as Christians is very different from theirs. Civic paganism is not an issue for us. We do not pass statues of pagan gods on our way into the mall, the hospital, or the tennis courts. Yet maybe a pagan statue or two at the entrance to the shopping center or the movie theater might serve a purpose. It would signal to us that modern society, like the ancient world, operates on some false assumptions about human nature and human happiness. Certainly American society mixes Christian and non-Christian values in confusing ways. And, like Christians in the past, we tend to be shaped by the prevailing values, good or bad. There is a Laodicean tendency in all of us.

John's letter and Polycarp's example point our attention to the root issues of personal allegiance and faithful service to Jesus in a culture where the current often flows in the opposite direction. Many of John's words and images may help us focus our reflections on these issues. Here are some suggestions:

The great white throne. The throne that John sees in heaven (4:2) represents God's ultimate authority over all. But each of us must choose whether to accept his authority. John is at pains to show the nothingness and evil of alternative gods. Nevertheless, we are free to choose them.

Earlier in my life, during a period of atheism, I was greatly helped by a Catholic friend who used a presentation developed by Protestant evangelist Bill Bright. My friend simply drew a circle with a throne in the middle of it. "The circle is your life," he said. "The question is, Who is on the throne? You? Your career? Your desire for experiences? Money? God?" That exercise focused my attention on the central issue I needed to face. Similarly, John's picture of the great white throne may help all of us reflect on this central question, which we must answer each day of our lives.

The bride of the Lamb. John's vision of the Church as the bride of Jesus (19:7–9; 21:2) carries a message of staggering importance for us. The creator of the universe invites each of us into a relationship of love and intimacy with him. The vision of the bride, then, also stands as a question. Am I growing in love for my Beloved today? When I face choices, do I remain faithful to my Beloved?

The beast. The beast reflects, at least to some extent, the climax of evil that John perceived in the Roman Empire, especially the veneration of the emperors as divine (12:3). While traditional paganism, with its images of gods, comes in for some criticism (9:20–21), John was most concerned about the problem of emperor worship.

Perhaps this is because the Roman emperors were acclaimed as benefactors of the world, the source of peace and prosperity for everyone. Such glorification of human beings is blasphemous—an act of supreme arrogance, a prideful attitude that shuts us off from God. As authors about the spiritual life constantly remind us, humility is the starting point for our relationship with God. The essence of humility, according to Dorotheos of Gaza, a seventh-century monk, is to ascribe everything good, including everything good in ourselves, to God. Blessed are those who recognize their poverty and need for God, Jesus declared (Matthew 5:3–4). Yet, as Scripture scholar Arthur Zannoni observes, there is something of the beast in all of us—a tendency to be proud, a tendency to deny or obscure our utter dependence on God. The image of the beast in Revelation poses questions to us: Who or what do I, perhaps unconsciously, regard as my source of life and goodness? What ultimately do I trust in? My own efforts? My education? My investments? My company? My doctor?

The crowd wearing white. The immense crowd of white-robed Christians John sees in heaven (7:9–17) are men and women who bore witness to Jesus in the world. They spoke of him in words and deeds.

On a visit to the United States, Pope John Paul II reminded American Christians that "the gospel of Jesus Christ is not a . . . mere program for personal growth. The gospel is the power which can transform the world! The gospel is . . . the living person of Jesus Christ, the Word of God, . . . the Incarnate Son who reveals the deepest meaning of our humanity and the noble destiny to which the whole human family is called. Christ commanded us to let the light of the gospel shine forth in our service to society. How can we profess faith in God's word, and then refuse to let it inspire and direct our thinking, our activity, our decisions, and our responsibilities toward one another?" This is the question posed to us by the vision of the white-robed witnesses.

The great whore. The prostitute is attractive, yet dangerous (17:2–4). She is the opposite of the bride of the Lamb. She especially represents self-indulgent materialism. Her image stands as a question to us about the degree to which we have let ourselves become caught up in the never-ending search for more goods and services. Her self-satisfaction leads us to ask ourselves, To what extent does my preoccupation with the material side of life deafen me to the needs of other people?

Of course, in our own time, other challenges to Christian values also need to be confronted. Again speaking in the United States, John Paul told Christians, "America faces a time of trial. The conflict is between a culture that affirms, cherishes, and celebrates the gift of life and a culture that seeks to declare entire groups of human beings—the unborn, the terminally ill, the handicapped—to be outside the boundaries of legal protection."

The Lord's Day. John received his visions on the Lord's Day, that is, Sunday (1:10), and his recipients would have read his letter when they gathered on the Lord's Day. Sunday was not a day off in the ancient world, so Christians had to meet before the beginning of the workday. They did so because they considered it essential to celebrate Jesus' resurrection together each week on that day. For them, celebrating the Lord's Day was countercultural.

Celebrating the Eucharist on the Lord's Day is becoming countercultural for us also. On the one hand, the weekend is now seen as a mainly secular leisure time. On the other hand, work and commercial activities encroach on Sunday. Will we, like our Christian ancestors, be countercultural and gather on the Lord's Day to celebrate Jesus' resurrection?

Suggestions for Bible Discussion Groups

L ike a camping trip, a Bible discussion group works best if you agree on what you're undertaking together, why you're doing it, where you hope to get to, and how you intend to get there. Many groups use their first meeting to reach a consensus on such questions. Here is a checklist of issues, with a few bits of advice from people with experience in Bible discussions. (A planning discussion will go more smoothly if the leaders have thought through the following issues beforehand.)

Agree on your purpose. Are you getting together to gain wisdom and direction for your life? to finally get acquainted with the Bible? to support one another in following Christ? to encourage those who are exploring—or reexploring—the Church? for other reasons?

Agree on attitudes. For example: "We're all beginners here." "We're here to help each other understand and respond to God's Word." "We're not here to offer counseling or direction to each other." "We want to read Scripture prayerfully." What do *you* wish to emphasize? Make it explicit!

Agree on ground rules. Barbara J. Fleischer, in her useful book *Facilitating for Growth,* recommends that a group clearly state its approach to the following:

✦ Preparation. Do we agree to read the material before each meeting?

✦ Attendance. What kind of priority will we give to our meetings?

✦ Self-revelation. Are we willing to help the others in the group gradually get to know us—our weaknesses as well as our strengths, our needs as well as our gifts?

✦ Listening. Will we commit ourselves to listening to each other?

✦ Confidentiality. Will we keep everything that is shared with the group in the group?

✦ Encouragement and support. Will we give as well as receive?

✦ Participation. Will we work to allow everyone time and opportunity to make a contribution?

You could probably take a pen and draw a circle around *listening* and *confidentiality.* Those two points are especially important.

The following items could be added to Fleischer's list:

✦ Relationship with parish. Is our group part of the religious education program? independent but operating with the express approval of the pastor? not a parish-based group at all?

✦ New members. In the course of the six meetings, will new members be allowed?

Agree on housekeeping.

✦ When will we meet?

✦ How often will we meet? Meeting weekly or every other week is best if you can manage it. William Riley remarks, "Meetings once a month are too distant from each other for the threads of the last session not to be lost" *(The Bible Study Group: An Owner's Manual).*

✦ How long will meetings run?

✦ Where will we meet?

✦ Is any setup needed? Christine Dodd writes that "the problem with meeting in a place like a church hall is that it can be very soul-destroying" given the cold, impersonal feel of many church facilities. If you have to meet in a church facility, Dodd recommends doing something to make the area homey *(Making Scripture Work).*

✦ Who will host the meetings? Leaders and hosts are not necessarily identical.

✦ Will we have refreshments? Who will provide them?

✦ What about child care? Most experienced leaders of Bible discussion groups discourage bringing infants or other children to adult Bible discussions.

Agree on leadership. You need someone to facilitate—to keep the discussion on track, to see that everyone has a chance to speak, to help the group stay on schedule. Rena Duff, editor of the newsletter *Sharing God's Word Today,* recommends having two or three people take turns leading the discussions.

It's okay if the leader is not an expert regarding the Bible. You have this booklet, and if questions come up that no one can answer, you can delegate a participant to do a little research between meetings. It's important for the leader to set an example of listening, to draw out the quieter members (and occasionally restrain the more vocal ones), to move the group on when it gets stuck, to remind the members of their agreements, and to sum-marize what the group is accomplishing.

Bible discussion is an opportunity to experience the fulfillment of Jesus' promise "Where two or three are gathered in my name, I am there among them" (Matthew 18:20). Put your discussion group in Jesus' hands. Pray for the guidance of the Spirit. And have a great time exploring God's Word together!

Suggestions for Individuals

You can use this booklet just as well for individual study as for group discussion. While discussing the Bible with other people can be a rich experience, there are advantages to individual reading. For example:

✦ You can focus on the points that interest you most.

✦ You can go at your own pace.

✦ You can be completely relaxed and unashamedly honest in your answers to all the questions, since you don't have to share them with anyone else!

My suggestions for using this booklet on your own are these:

✦ Don't skip the "Questions to Begin." The questions can help you as an individual reader warm up to the topic of the reading.

✦ Take your time on "Questions for Careful Reading" and "Questions for Application." While a group will probably not have enough time to work on all the questions, you can allow yourself the time to consider all of them if you are using the booklet by yourself.

✦ If you are going through Revelation at your own pace, consider reading the entire book, not just the parts excerpted in this booklet. "Between Discussions" pages will give you some guidance in reading the additional portions of Revelation. Your total understanding of John's letter will be greatly increased by reading through Revelation from beginning to end.

✦ Since you control the pace, give yourself plenty of opportunities to reflect on the meaning of Revelation for you. Let your reading be an opportunity for John's words to become God's words to you.

Bibles

The following editions of the Bible contain the full set of biblical books recognized by the Catholic Church, along with a great deal of useful explanatory material:

✦ The Catholic Study Bible (Oxford University Press), which uses the text of the New American Bible

✦ The Catholic Bible: Personal Study Edition (Oxford University Press), which also uses the text of the New American Bible

✦ The New Jerusalem Bible, the regular (not the reader's) edition (Doubleday)

Books

✦ *The Book of Revelation*, The Navarre Bible (Dublin: Four Courts Press, 1992).

✦ G. B. Caird, *The Revelation of Saint John*, Black's New Testament Commentary (Peabody, Mass.: Hendrickson Publishers, 1966).

✦ Wilfrid J. Harrington, O.P., *Revelation*, Sacra Pagina (Collegeville, Minn.: Liturgical Press, 1993).

✦ George T. Montague, S.M., *The Apocalypse: Understanding the Book of Revelation and the End of the World* (Ann Arbor, Mich.: Servant Publications, 1992).

How has Scripture had an impact on your life? Was this booklet helpful to you in your study of the Bible? Please send comments, suggestions, and personal experiences to Kevin Perrotta c/o Trade Editorial Department, Loyola Press, 3441 N. Ashland Ave., Chicago, IL 60657.